Introducing Shakespeare's Tragedies

Introducing Shakespeare's Tragedies

A Guide for Teachers

Victor L. Cahn

ROWMAN & LITTLEFIELD
Lanham • Boulder • New York • London

Published by Rowman & Littlefield
A wholly owned subsidiary of The Rowman & Littlefield Publishing Group, Inc.
4501 Forbes Boulevard, Suite 200, Lanham, Maryland 20706
www.rowman.com

Unit A, Whitacre Mews, 26-34 Stannary Street, London SE11 4AB

Copyright © 2017 by Victor L. Cahn

All rights reserved. No part of this book may be reproduced in any form or by any electronic or mechanical means, including information storage and retrieval systems, without written permission from the publisher, except by a reviewer who may quote passages in a review.

British Library Cataloguing in Publication Information Available

Library of Congress Cataloging-in-Publication Data

Names: Cahn, Victor L. author.
Title: Introducing Shakespeare's tragedies : a guide for teachers / Victor L. Cahn.
Description: Lanham : Rowman & Littlefield, 2017. | Includes bibliographical references.
Identifiers: LCCN 2017019725 (print) | LCCN 2017031365 (ebook) | ISBN 9781475836110 (electronic) | ISBN 9781475836097 (cloth : alk. paper) | ISBN 9781475836103 (pbk. : alk. paper)
Subjects: LCSH: Shakespeare, William, 1564–1616--Study and teaching. | Shakespeare, William, 1564–1616—Tragedies.
Classification: LCC PR2987 (ebook) | LCC PR2987 .C36 2017 (print) | DDC 822.3/3—dc23 LC record available at https://lccn.loc.gov/2017019725

Printed in the United States of America

To the memory of my mother,
Evelyn Baum Cahn,
who taught these plays many years ago.

Contents

Preface	ix
Introduction	xi
A Few Words About the Tragedies	1
1 *Romeo and Juliet*	5
2 *Julius Caesar*	17
3 *Hamlet*	29
4 *Othello*	45
5 *King Lear*	61
6 *Macbeth*	83
Afterword	101
About the Author	103

Preface

For forty years I taught the plays of Shakespeare, and the more I taught and wrote about them, the more fascinating they became. Now I'd like to share some of what I learned with my fellow instructors in the hope of aiding those at the junior high school, high school, and undergraduate levels who offer some of Shakespeare's most familiar works to students who are largely unfamiliar with them.

I've divided my material into two books: one on the tragedies, the other on the comedies, histories, and romances. Each volume begins with a general introduction intended for any teacher preparing to present any play in the canon. This section includes biographical material on Shakespeare, information about the world of the theater in which he flourished, and perspective on the intellectual underpinnings of his time. Not everything here will be appropriate for every instructor, but I like to think that most will find something of value in my cursory overview.

I then move to a baker's dozen of Shakespeare's plays, all of which have inspired enthusiastic response from classes. Although I assume that my readers have already experienced the works, I proceed through each as if an audience was encountering it for the first time. Because these analyses can only broach the wealth of discussion suggested by the texts, my strategy is to propose what actors and directors sometimes refer to as the "spine" of the play: an overarching conflict or motivation that I embellish with specifics. Thus when quoting, I rarely reprint entire passages. Instead I focus on crucial sections and trust that my colleagues will help students delve more deeply.

This effort leads to the most challenging aspect of Shakespeare's plays: the language. Both the poetry and prose are extraordinary but also multilayered and sometimes archaic, and students are likely to be unaccustomed to probing words as closely as Shakespeare demands. As a result, many will resort to editions in which the dialogue is "translated" into modern English, but part of our job is to ensure that even those who avail themselves of such tools still appreciate the original.

Therefore, during sessions students should keep the text in front of them, and teachers should constantly direct attention to specific lines. These should be read out loud, by either the instructor or the students, because Shakespeare's words were meant to be heard, not seen. In addition, even though we devote considerable class time to explicating this complex material, students still deserve assurance that even if they (like almost all of us) don't understand every word, they can still grasp the beauty and power of Shakespeare's writing.

My overall aim is to analyze how these plays succeed as theater. Decades ago, to help achieve that end, I brought recordings to class, then in later years moved to VHSs and DVDs. Now multiple performances are available on the web, and all of us can watch at our own convenience. I still suggest, though, that students first read the play under discussion, then turn to a video because the combination of sight and sound should make the deepest impression. No doubt these plays are most effective in performance, but I'm also convinced that under the guidance of a skillful teacher, they may prove compelling in the classroom, as well.

All quotations are taken from the Folger Shakespeare Library editions.

My thanks to Tom Koerner and Emily Tuttle of Rowman & Littlefield, who have supported this project from the start, as well as my production editor, Lara Hahn, who diligently prepared the manuscript.

My gratitude as always to my brother, Dr. Steven M. Cahn, my trusted guide on all matters scholarly and otherwise.

Introduction

William Shakespeare was above all a man of the theater, and he was fortunate that his creative life coincided with an era when English drama thrived. His oeuvre, though, was part of a tradition that extended back through the Middle Ages, when plays were presented by itinerant performers. Gradually these groups were replaced by professional companies, stimulated by the ever-growing market for entertainment in London, the capital of the country and its economic, political, and social center.

Theater of that time benefitted from a confluence of other forces. By 1558, when Elizabeth I ascended the throne, the spirit of the Renaissance had brought renewed interest in classical literature, specifically Roman playwrights like Terence and Plautus, writers of comedy, and Seneca, author of numerous tragedies, and these figures became models for young dramatists. Furthermore, professional companies were sanctioned, while theater continued to burgeon in academic institutions and private halls. Public performances were given in innyards, where galleries were built to hold spectators.

These companies were infused with university graduates, most notably Christopher Marlowe, like Shakespeare born in 1564. The author of several masterpieces, including *Dr. Faustus*, Marlowe spent his life in notorious circles and was killed in a tavern brawl before the age of thirty. Nevertheless, his distinctive variety of blank verse, sometimes called the "mighty line," contributed enormously to the poetic style that shaped drama, including Shakespeare's, for decades.

Meanwhile, acting companies remained under attack by the Puritans, who condemned theater not only because it ostensibly contributed to moral dissolution but also because performances interfered with business. In addition, given that theater companies functioned in unsavory areas, the lord mayor and his counsel objected for reasons of both health and decorum. Thus in

1574, decrees were passed so that no plays could be presented within city limits unless scripts, as well as times and places of performance, were officially approved. In reaction, acting companies built playhouses just outside the municipality, and here they prospered until 1642, when the Puritans closed operations entirely.

Shakespeare joined this world in approximately 1590, when he was in his mid-twenties. His own education had been limited to grammar school in his birthplace of Stratford, where he was one of eight children born to John and Mary Shakespeare. John was a glover who enjoyed some good fortune but also suffered severe financial setbacks, so young Shakespeare must have known both a degree of comfort as well as the pangs and humiliations of poverty. He also seems to have had a remarkable memory for the sights, sounds, and smells of his hometown.

By the way, members of the group known as the anti-Stratfordians claim that the individual known as William Shakespeare could not have written the body of work attributed to him. The primary reason is that an untutored fellow was incapable of producing such masterpieces, and among the other candidates are the Earl of Oxford, Marlowe, and Queen Elizabeth herself. Without going into the vast body of evidence that supports the view that the man from Stratford wrote these plays (notably that almost everybody else proposed as author was dead when the works appeared), let's assume that they are his and move on.

As a schoolboy, William endured lengthy hours in a classroom whose curriculum was heavily weighted with Latin literature, including the writings of Cicero, Horace, Virgil, and Ovid, and proof of such study may be found throughout Shakespeare's writings. Recitation was a bulwark of instruction, and no doubt emphasis on articulation and rhythmic precision gave Shakespeare affection for both the glories of language and the delights of performance. He also read intensively in Roman history, and some of the lessons he learned emerge in his Roman plays and his sequences about English history.

In 1582, Shakespeare married Anne Hathaway, eight years his senior and several months pregnant with their first child. Within three years, the couple had three children: Susanna, born in 1583, and twins Hamnet and Judith, born in 1585. Hamnet would die at age eleven. The seven years following the birth of his twins are the so-called lost years because documentary evidence about Shakespeare's activities is limited. Speculation holds that he may have been a schoolmaster, a provincial actor, or a lawyer's assistant. He may also have spent time on the Continent.

By 1592, however, he must have been established in London, for he was alluded to disparagingly by playwright Robert Greene. In an attack on actors in general, Greene refers to "Shake-scene," then to an "upstart crow" with "his Tyger's hart wrapt in a Player's hyde [*sic*]."

The last parodies a line from *Henry VI, Part 3*: "O, tiger's heart wrapped in a woman's hide" (1, 4, 140). Greene may have been intimating that Shakespeare was a plagiarist or merely that the young man was presumptuous. Whatever the implication, the reference shows that Shakespeare was well known enough to be obliquely criticized.

In 1592, an outbreak of bubonic plague struck the city, and for two years theaters were closed. When they reopened in 1594, Shakespeare, as actor and playwright, joined a new company called the Lord Chamberlain's Men under the auspices of an aristocratic personage who provided artistic and economic protection. During the rest of the 1590s, the company rented theaters, but by 1599 the Globe Theater had been constructed, and here is where most performances of Shakespeare's plays were presented. In 1623, after James I became king, the name was changed to the King's Men.

Thus for a substantial time Shakespeare enjoyed a creative environment that playwrights have always relished: the opportunity to write for a resident company of capable and experienced actors, with their own facilities at the ready. Had he lived in another era, he might have written 154 sonnets and several longer poems, but he almost certainly would not have written the 37 plays that remain celebrated.

Theatrical conditions helped shape the dramatic works of this day. In most theaters, the stage, a covered platform without curtains, extended into the audience. Toward the rear of the stage was a higher level that could serve as a balcony or "battlement," from which actors could look down on the action below. Most of the theaters were open-air constructions, round or hexagonal, and of considerable size. The Globe itself could hold two thousand spectators. Yet the houses encouraged intimacy between audience and actor, so that asides and soliloquies became a valuable method of communication.

In most public theaters, two or three tiers of seats were provided for the well-to-do, who sometimes overflowed onto the stage. Here they tended to behave somewhat disreputably in an effort to draw attention to themselves. Below the stage, in the pit, stood or sat the less wealthy citizens, known as the "groundlings," and they were an impatient, demanding group. Yet they were also appreciative and when moved by what they saw and heard, were prone to cheering, shouting, and crying.

Perhaps because Shakespeare's audience encompassed so wide a range of people, he created equally heterogeneous rosters of characters, from the highest echelons of society to the very bottom, and placed them in a variety of locales, settings, and moods. He also moved regularly from comedy to history to tragedy, triumphing in each form with a virtuosity unmatched by any other dramatist before or since.

Most of Shakespeare's works were written for public theaters, and their technical deficiencies also influenced his writing. Perhaps needless to say, artificial lighting was not available, so performances took place in the daytime and without intermissions. Division of the plays into separate acts was accomplished by later editors, and therefore audience attention must have been considerable. Granted, few other entertainments were available: church services, executions, and bear baiting, to name some of the most prominent. Thus theater was a welcome alternative. Nonetheless, to hold audience focus, a premium was placed on continual action.

Costumes were extravagant and helped define character in terms of nationality and class. Scenery, however, was minimal, and flats, curtains, and simple wooden structures had to suffice to represent houses and other edifices. Props were strictly for efficacy. Programs were not available, so the text itself had to identify characters and establish locales. Hence Shakespeare's poetic renderings of environment were not just for the sake of beauty but also to communicate the texture of a forest or castle that had to be suggested rather than re-created.

Battles between massive armies were enacted by a few performers dashing about the stage with swords. Although trapdoors and such devices as sound and visual effects were available to simulate supernatural and other spectacular displays, the unceasing movement in Shakespeare's plays, the energy we as yet admire, was demanded by the conditions under which he worked.

Theatrical conditions also imposed demands on the actors. The turnover of plays was steady, and parts had to be learned after only a few rehearsals and with little direction (and while actors were performing in other works). Thus their capacity for memorization must have been astonishing. Yet we should remember the nature of elementary education in England at this time. The primary activity was rote training, and at a very early age students were drilled into retaining long poems and prose passages. (For confirmation, ask your students how many remember whatever material they memorized during their initial academic years.)

Acting itself was carried out with vigor and passion, tending toward the declamatory. Again, to state the obvious, no microphones or other methods for projection were available. Indeed, Shakespeare's taste for what in our day would be described as "chewing the scenery" may be seen in Hamlet's instructions to the players in 3, 2. The most famous members of Shakespeare's company were Richard Burbage, who gave the premiere performances of most of Shakespeare's great tragic roles, and Will Kemp, a gifted comic star whose liberties onstage antagonized his colleagues and led to his dismissal.

Shakespeare himself also appeared onstage, generally in smaller roles and often as older men. He may have been the Chorus in *Henry V*, apologizing for the limits of his writing, and he may have played the Ghost in *Hamlet*. No matter the extent of his contributions as a thespian, however; his primary task was to write, and he did so with unmatched success. Contemporary reports indicate that productions of his works were successful and that no matter his actors' deficiencies, Shakespeare was well served.

The most important limitation on the playwright was the absence of actresses. Although women were permitted to perform on the Continent, the English judged such practice as immoral, and from medieval times all female roles were played by boys. One consequence of this restriction was that the parts Shakespeare wrote for males outnumber those for females by five or six to one.

A couple of these boys must have been talented, for many of Shakespeare's comedies contain prominent roles for pairs of young women. In addition, Shakespeare frequently arranges for one or both to disguise themselves as men. The impersonation is always successful, but even given that ploy, the capacity of his audience to accept the illusion of boys playing girls must have been remarkable.

To be sure, the plays generally lack extended female parts, especially for mature women, because boys could not carry off a role as complex as Othello or Lear. Late in his career, however, Shakespeare must have found at least one young male in whom he had confidence because he created Lady Macbeth, Cleopatra, and other roles whose demands match those of his greatest male parts.

For nearly twenty years, from the early 1590s until 1611, Shakespeare wrote an average of two plays a year, and the steadiness of his output suggests that he had little time for revision. Thus what have been passed down to us may not be precisely first drafts, but surely the speeches and pages flowed easily from his quill. In contrast to later dramatists, Shakespeare wrote strictly for performance and most likely without an eye toward publication. In fact, only about half his plays were printed individually during his lifetime.

The playwright seems to have paid little attention to textual accuracy. Laws of the day gave him no copyright control, so prompters, actors, other playwrights, and even company bookkeepers could make changes that satisfied their needs. Besides, once plays were published, they were no longer the province of an individual company, which would lose a valuable commodity when a popular script was available to rival groups.

Fortunately, in 1623, seven years after Shakespeare's death, two of his former colleagues collected thirty-six of his plays in a single volume known as the First Folio (*Pericles* is omitted). Here the plays are classified as tragedies, histories, and comedies. This text is the basis for virtually all editions currently used, but innumerable questions about authenticity remain. Many different editors worked on the volume, so some copies of the folio are at variance with others. Words, stage directions, spelling, and even entire passages are all open to question.

No single book on Shakespeare can encompass all perspectives from which the plays may be considered. This book is based on a traditional conviction: that the core of their impact lies with the characters. So lifelike are they that although they are set in ages long past, we are inspired to explore them as we would real human beings. We may struggle to resolve some of their seemingly contradictory actions and statements, but these can almost always be synthesized into what actors designate as a "through line," a consistent path of motivation.

Dramatic figures, like people, reveal themselves through language and action. We analyze them not only by what they do but also by what they say and how they say it. Two precepts apply here. One, the language a speaker uses, taken in concert with the speaker's actions, reveals the speaker's character, while the richness of the language reflects the depth of that character. Two, how that character reacts to circumstances of plot reveals theme.

Attempting to analyze language in these plays can be daunting. First, many of Shakespeare's words are no longer part of our vocabulary. Second, other words seem familiar, but their meaning may have changed drastically since he penned them. Third, pronunciation may also have altered, so that we are not aware of potential homonyms (words that sound alike) or puns. Fourth, to enrich his dialogue, Shakespeare uses not only metaphors and similes, as well as numerous other forms of imagery, but also a variety of poetic and rhetorical devices that can make the immediate meaning problematic.

Individual lines can also create difficulties. Roughly three-quarters of Shakespeare's dialogue is blank verse or unrhymed iambic pentameter. An iamb consists of one short syllable followed by one long one or one unaccented syllable followed by one accented one; for example, "da-DUM." Pentameter refers to a line with five such beats. Sometimes the iambic verse is rhymed, usually when the speaker wants to project artificiality. Thus rhymed couplets appear in asides, declarations of love, or other contexts requiring a linguistic flair. Speakers may also use prose, which is offered in less formal circumstances or by less exalted characters.

We should remember that although Shakespeare's characters reveal aspects of humanity at large, they themselves function during a specific time and in a specific place. Thus they should be seen as reflecting aspects of the culture in which they were created. Elizabethan England was primarily Christian, and its view of the world followed generally from a medieval vision. This held that the universe was created by God as a perfect work, a unity in which every aspect of creation had its place.

This "great chain of being" encompassed all, from the lowest inanimate objects to the angels, placing each in what were judged to be natural places of subordination. Humankind occupied a unique place, for the human animal possessed both soul and body and therefore endured a conflict between its divine capacity, or reason, and its base appetites, or passions. Any imperfections in the world were caused by humanity, not God.

Within this system was a series of correspondences. As God was the highest among the angels, so the sun was the highest among the stars, fire the highest of the elements, the king the highest among human beings, and so on. In addition, a fundamental relationship existed between the macrocosm and the microcosm. God was ruler of the universe, the macrocosm, as a monarch was ruler of the political structure, the microcosm. Any disorder in the social microcosm created repercussions that extended into the macrocosm.

Order in the political realm corresponded to order in the human body. Just as the surrounding world, the macrocosm, was said to be composed of four elements (fire, air, water, and earth), so the human microcosm contained four parallel humors (choler, blood, phlegm, and melancholy). Any imbalance of these within an individual could lead to disorder that extended into the political plane and even into the universal plane. Finally, we have to keep in mind that this medieval vision was tempered by the influence of the Renaissance and the Reformation.

The Renaissance (literally, "rebirth") was an age during which leading thinkers believed they were inspiring a return to the human and earthly concerns of the pagan classical world. In addition to celebrating this artistic heritage, the fourteenth and fifteenth centuries saw the development of a money economy, with increased opportunity for individual trade and profit. At the same time, urban populations grew, and intellectual life in the universities expanded, while scientific inquiry and a resultant skepticism emerged.

The European Reformation, based primarily on religious motives, took some authority away from the church by insisting on a personal relationship between each human being and God. In England, the Reformation followed Henry VIII's rift with the Catholic Church over his divorce. Attendance in the new Church of England was still enforced, but now, the English monarch also held authority over religious matters, and the psychological fulcrum that the Catholic Church had provided for centuries was splintered.

These two powerful movements held some conflicting values. While the Renaissance reveled in the possibilities of secular daily life, the Reformation emphasized individual piety and an overwhelming concern for the afterlife. Renaissance humanism judged human nature to be fundamentally benign, while according to the Reformation, humanity was essentially depraved. The Renaissance advocated reason; the Reformation sought to impose faith and conformity.

Yet the Renaissance and Reformation had equally important values in common. Both emerged from a mercantile system based on capitalism and an ever-developing and prosperous middle class. Both shook the image of the world as a static entity, and each in its own way shifted responsibility toward the individual. This new perspective gave rise to new freedoms but also to new uncertainties.

In England, the rise of the gentry reflected alienation from a feudal system to one based on private enterprise. The nation was beset by a series of intellectual and moral crises springing from disputes over political rights, social rights, and the seemingly heretical results of scientific discovery, such as those by Copernicus and Galileo. In addition, awareness of new lands and societies, especially throughout the Americas, caused European civilization to reflect on the very nature of the human species, as well as on fundamental questions of morality and theology.

All this turmoil was reflected in the central subject of Elizabethan literature: the struggle for stability between individual lives and the social order. Shakespeare's plays, too, dramatize this tension between old and new, between the world as a closed, structured system and the power of individuals to find their own way. The plays celebrate individuality but at the same time reflect the belief that the assertion of an individual's will creates conflict. For when that will is exercised, whether in the malevolent desire for power or wealth or a beneficent desire for love, equilibrium within the individual is upset.

This imbalance in Shakespeare's characters is always the mainspring of the plot, the force that propels the action. In the comedies and certain romances, personal imbalance tends to remain localized. In Shakespeare's tragedies, histories, and other romances, it occurs within individuals of such magnitude that their actions have ramifications that spread throughout the social, political, and even universal structure.

Virtually all of Shakespeare's plots are borrowed from earlier sources. Whatever the story, though, all of Shakespeare's plays end with the reestablishment of personal and political order. Such restoration reflects the essential conservatism of both the age and the playwright, but Shakespeare's conservatism is profoundly humanitarian. Even at his most pessimistic, when cruelty and heartbreak seem overwhelming, these resolutions communicate faith in humanity and the universe. Such sympathy underlies even his most villainous characters, and our embracing of them testifies to the genius of their creator.

William Shakespeare died on April 23, 1616, the anniversary, according to tradition, of his birth fifty-three years earlier. Over his grave in Stratford Church are these words:

> Good friend for Jesus' sake forbear
> To dig the dust enclosed here.
> Blessed be the man that spares these stones,
> And cursed be he that moves these bones.

An even more famous tribute was offered by Shakespeare's contemporary, the eminent poet and playwright Ben Jonson:

> Triumph, my Britain, thou hast one to show

> To whom all scenes of Europe homage owe.
> He was not of an age, but for all time!

Indeed, Jonson's words have proven prophetic. Across the centuries and all national boundaries, Shakespeare's works have remained at the forefront, and only the Bible has been translated into more languages. The plays have been produced in virtually every society, and each audience, whether Western or Eastern, agrarian or industrialized, finds its own themes and values in them.

Nonetheless, the texts have not always been treated reverently. From 1642 through the early 1660s, when the Puritans ruled England, theaters were shut. But when the English monarchy was restored and theaters were reopened, new technical facilities were developed. More elaborate lighting and moveable scenery allowed for all sorts of realistic as well as pyrotechnical effects. Women were at last allowed to take to the stage, and thus the convention of young males in female parts disappeared.

At the same time, many scripts, including those of Shakespeare, were subject to ruthless revision that suited the tastes of the era. The most notorious rewriting was Nahum Tate's 1681 version of *King Lear*. In the eighteenth century, texts were subject to less abuse, and acting became we might call more realistic or natural. Still, satisfying audience taste remained the primary motivation, and even the supreme actor David Garrick tried his hand at rewriting *Romeo and Juliet* by creating a version in which the title characters are reunited before their deaths.

Despite such abuse, Shakespeare continues to thrive. For actors and directors, the plays remain the supreme test of skill and imagination and encourage inexhaustible approaches to production. In an attempt to achieve authenticity, contemporary companies have reverted to all-male presentations, joined recently by all-female ones. In virtually every state in our country, and in virtually every country around the world, Shakespeare festivals abound. No other dramatist receives a modicum of such attention.

Over the centuries, stories from the plays have been transformed into countless adaptations and retellings, including films, operas, symphonic portraits, ballets, and musical comedies, as well as stage productions that are veritable riffs off the formal script. Thanks to video recordings, performances that once might have disappeared forever are now available at the touch of a computer screen.

Countless eloquent and insightful lines from his plays and poetry are now an indelible part of world culture. In any book of famous quotations, samples from even the most eminent authors cover no more than a few pages. Inevitably the two largest sections, often set apart from the rest of the compilation, are devoted to the Bible and Shakespeare, with thousands of citations from each.

The popularity and influence of Shakespeare's work has inevitably given rise to critical analysis, and the staggering volume of material grows exponentially every year. No writer has been the subject of such intense study, and the multitude of critical perspectives testifies to the richness of the material, even as they reveal the critics' prejudices and limitations.

Earliest commentators focused on Shakespeare as a natural genius, whose lack of formal training led to tendencies in plot structure and character that violated long-standing "rules" of dramaturgy. By the end of the eighteenth century, concern moved away from the dictates of formality to what was to become the object of scrutiny for the next century: Shakespeare's profound understanding of humanity. The poet Samuel Taylor Coleridge emphasized that although Shakespeare deviated from the classical unities of time, place, and action, his plays held together because of unity of feeling.

During the past century, preoccupations of our era have been mirrored in attitudes toward art, and the plays of Shakespeare have been examined as closely as any works in any form. Schools of criticism now conjecture whether a single "reading" of a play is even possible or whether all interpretation is dependent on the nature and response of the audience, as well as the social, political, and economic environment in which the play is experienced.

With acknowledgment of such trends, we shall forge ahead, buttressed by two thoughts that are helpful to pose before a class begins to read anything by Shakespeare. One is best expressed by holding up a volume of the collected plays and announcing that this book is the greatest that any one person has ever written. The other is quoted by James Joyce in *Ulysses*, citing the words of Alexandre Dumas, père: "After God, Shakespeare created the most."

A Few Words About the Tragedies

These works are the ones with which students are most likely to be familiar, if only by reputation, and that knowledge will help guide their way into reading. Yet the very word *tragedies* implies that the experience will be grim, so arousing interest will not be easy. Still, the power of these plays is irresistible, and with the right approach they can inspire a class as few activities can.

Begin by explaining that the tragic form is perhaps the noblest dramatic expression of the human predicament. At its core is the conflict of a hero or heroine against overwhelming odds, a conflict that always ends in catastrophe. Part of the struggle these characters face is an attempt to find meaning in existence, but questions about the nature of suffering or the origins of evil remain beyond understanding, and the death of the tragic protagonist is the inevitable price of challenge and failure. Nevertheless, the battle so ennobles these figures that their efforts dignify humankind.

Next, consider the concept of Shakespearean tragedy. It covers a wide range of plays, and to establish one all-encompassing definition is impossible. Certainly the works do not conform to a single set of principles, such as those proposed by Aristotle as an ideal to which Greek tragedy should aspire. Yet most of Shakespeare's tragic dramas share several qualities that we can delineate.

One, the central figure undergoes conflict against the social order. Contrast this structure with the predicament of heroes and heroines from Greek tragedy, who battle divine forces. In Sophocles's *Oedipus the King*, for instance (a play students might know), the title character is condemned by the gods to kill his father and marry his mother. No matter what he does, he cannot escape this destiny. He is not, however, fated to discover that he has in fact committed these crimes, and thus tension arises from two forces:

Oedipus's own character, which drives him to learn that he is the man who has brought a plague on Thebes; and his realization of what he has done and the burden of how he will live with that knowledge.

Two, in Shakespeare's tragedies, divine beings do not determine human action. To be sure, some characters speak of fate or destiny, and in several plays individuals look to the heavens for explanation of unhappy events or to avoid responsibility for them. But never do we feel that outside forces control characters. In Shakespeare, the cause of human suffering is human action, and we are always conscious that human beings are free to choose their paths. Here is one reason that even though the plays of Shakespeare are set in distant times and places, the works still touch us.

Are the choices that characters make in any way limited? Yes, but the limitations come from within characters themselves. All tragic figures in Shakespeare face extraordinary crises, and their exquisite dilemma is that the qualities of greatness that make the characters worthy of their position militate against successful resolution of these crises. In other words, the attributes that elevate these characters to great heights are the very ones that pull them down to the most profound depths.

This last claim requires textual support, but even at first glance it should make sense. After all, the essence of drama is tension between an intriguing, even problematic personality and a tantalizing situation that compels that personality to grapple with itself. In Shakespeare's plays, we find this mixture brought together by the most gifted dramatic hand the human race has produced.

Such interaction between character and circumstance especially enriches these plays when we know information that the characters do not. The result is dramatic irony, as individuals follow what we are aware is a disastrous course of action. A variety of movie scenes may help elucidate this concept. Describe one where a courageous protagonist walks toward a door behind which we see the murderer, or where a misguided protagonist confides in someone who has proven to be an enemy, or where a confident protagonist boasts about being safe while we see a hidden bomb about to explode. Students will surely supply their own.

Note, too, that although these plays present human characters and human events as the springboard of conflict, that focus does not eliminate the mystery of experience. Here good and evil clash, but the reasons are not always evident. To make this idea more vivid, select some event from the news or from history that left people asking something to the effect of "How could this happen?" or "How could someone behave this way?" Unfortunately, examples will be all too easy to find.

Finally, in experiencing these works, we ponder the nature of the human animal, a nature that permits moments of exultation but also seems to make suffering endemic to our lives. This uncertainty is balanced by trust in the human spirit. Such faith emerges not only because at the end of each of Shakespeare's tragedies, the value of goodness is affirmed but also because the plays themselves reflect how human existence, through the prism of artistic expression, inspires passion and wonder.

Chapter One

Romeo and Juliet

As discussed in chapter 1 on *The Taming of the Shrew* in *Introducing Shakespeare's Comedies, Histories, and Romances: A Guide for Teachers*, *Romeo and Juliet* is one of the two archetypal love stories. The pattern is that of two strangers who catch each other's eye and draw together. All would be ideal except for interference by either outside forces, such as their families, or interior conflicts within the characters themselves. Asking the class for examples of the genre will guarantee responses ranging from episodes of countless television series to the musical *West Side Story*, so the universal attraction of the story will quickly become apparent.

The best place to begin is the opening sonnet delivered by the Chorus. The first five lines reveal the core of the plot: Two families are at war, and as a result two young people will die. The key words are *fatal* (Prologue, 5) and *star-crossed* (Prologue, 6). Do they imply that providence is in control? We are told the outcome of events to follow. Are human choice and responsibility consequently irrelevant? Does our knowledge of the ending preclude all excitement and wonder?

If fate is in charge, then this play is singular in the Shakespearean canon. Therefore encourage students to think of fate as a combination of the weight of the past plus pressure from the present environment. Given this society, the natures of the characters, and the intensity of their love, no other outcome is possible. As the story unwinds, we find ourselves rooting for another ending, but the play suggests that the human personality is helpless against itself. Character is destiny, a fair estimate not only of this play but of all Shakespeare's plays.

Remember, too, that the surrounding forces are human: "civil blood makes civil hands unclean" (Prologue, 4). Although at moments chance and coincidence seem to intrude, from the start we are directed toward human interference: "The fearful passage of their death-marked love / And the continuance of their parents' rage" (Prologue, 9–10). We are never told the origin of this feud. All we learn is that human fallibility wreaks havoc with human aspiration.

In adopting this story from a poem by Arthur Brooke, Shakespeare made several significant changes. One, he compacted months into four days, reflecting the intensity of youthful love. Two, he developed the character of Mercutio. Three, Shakespeare emphasizes the purity of the love affair and the boldness of the lovers' disobedience against their parents. Four, Shakespeare's Juliet is loving and honest, while Romeo is more than just a stereotypical lover. Finally, while Brooke depicts the lovers' deaths as punishment warranted by their sins, Shakespeare glorifies their love.

The action proper begins in the street, where servants from the two families, the Capulets and the Montagues, exchange threats and sexual puns, such as those about "maidenheads" (1, 1, 26) or "my naked weapon" (1, 1, 34). These are the first in a play filled with them, especially when Mercutio talks. How to handle this material depends on the maturity of the students and the discretion of the teacher, but in any case be prepared.

Matters become more serious when Tybalt enters, scorning talk of peace: "I hate the word / As I hate hell, all Montagues, and thee" (1, 1, 71–72). The violence inspires even old Capulet, who comically tries to enter the fray, only to be restrained by his wife, just as Montague's wife muzzles him. Hereafter we are conscious that incipient male violence threatens the stability of Verona. These exchanges also suggest that had the playwright chosen another direction, the play might have turned into a comedy like *A Midsummer Night's Dream*, written during the same period.

The disorder halts with the intrusion of Prince Escalus, who clarifies that this private squabble hurts the city at large (1, 1, 91–97). He also specifies the families' crime: that from an excess of fervor, they have created havoc, a proclivity within several characters to be dramatized later. He then threatens both families with an ultimatum that hangs over the subsequent action: "If you ever disturb our streets again, / Your lives shall pay the forfeit of the peace" (1, 1, 98–99). From this point on, we suspect that at least one character will perpetrate violence that endangers lives.

Immediately we hear about Romeo, reported by Benvolio to be in the throes of romance: "Many a morning hath he there been seen, / With tears augmenting the fresh morning's dew" (1, 1, 134–35). Shakespeare's audience would have recognized this description as fitting a typical young man in love. Soon Romeo reinforces that impression: "Why then, O brawling love, O loving hate, / O anything of nothing first create" (1, 1, 181–82), The awkward rhythms and oxymora (contrasting words in one image) reveal someone more in love with love than with anyone else.

The action moves swiftly to the house of Capulet, where Paris receives permission to court Juliet, not quite fourteen (1, 2, 9). Paris is an innocuous young man, but because he has been selected by Juliet's father, we may not sympathize with him. At least, however, Capulet wants her to marry someone she loves (1, 2, 17–19). Thus at this juncture, Capulet is not a villain, but his exertion of authority still annoys us.

What follows is the first of several coincidences. A servant is ordered to invite various personages to a party at the Capulet home, but the illiterate man, unable to decipher the list of guests, runs into Romeo and Benvolio and asks them to read for him. When Romeo finds the name of his current love, Rosaline, he resolves to attend. Is this chance meeting the result of fate? Not at all. Instead our attention should remain on Romeo and his impulsiveness in going where he is not welcome. Note, too, that Rosaline never appears, so we never contrast her with the woman with whom Romeo becomes enamored.

Scene 3 introduces the Nurse who cares for Juliet. The figure of the lusty older woman is a staple of comedy, and the Nurse's bawdy language helps her fulfill that role: "'Thou wilt fall backward when thou hast more wit, / Wilt thou not, Jule?'" (1, 3, 46–47). She is not, however, the only clever one onstage, as Juliet suggests when she answers her mother's question about marriage to Paris: "It is an honor I dream not of" (1, 3, 71). Such modesty disguises the implication that Juliet prefers to choose her own husband, but her mother misses that insinuation, as does the Nurse, who instead focuses on Paris's good looks (1, 3, 82).

Lady Capulet, too, wants the best for her daughter and, like the Nurse, appreciates appearance. Even so, her love for Juliet confirms that this play does not have a villain. Instead, characters who mean well intrude on Romeo and Juliet, whose love is conducted on such an exalted plane that it must topple when forced to conform to the values of the surrounding society. Most of the characters have only good intentions, yet these prove inadequate.

This phenomenon is embodied by Mercutio, who takes over this scene as well as the play. Romeo understands Mercutio's magnetism:

> You have dancing shoes
> With nimble soles. I have a soul of lead
> So stakes me to the ground I cannot move. (1, 4, 14–16)

In return, Mercutio understands that he is all flash with little substance but that his younger friend has a different manner: "You are a lover. Borrow Cupid's wings / And soar with them above a common bound" (1, 4, 17–18). Mercutio seems a couple of years older than Romeo, who is usually taken to be about seventeen.

The essence of Mercutio (said to be modeled on Shakespeare's rival Christopher Marlowe) is his lustiness: "Prick love for pricking, and you beat love down" (1, 4, 28). The most compelling manifestation of his spirit is the famous "Queen Mab" speech. It begins with the brilliant description of a fantasy world in which Mab fulfills the dreamer's greatest desire (1, 4, 58–79), but degenerates into violence and ugly sexuality:

> This is the hag, when maids lie on their backs,
> That presses them and learns them first to bear,
> Making them women of good carriage. (1, 4, 97–99)

Mercutio is likewise a dreamer who hides his latent fury. Yet whatever his attractiveness, Romeo tires of the barrage: "Peace, peace, Mercutio, peace. / Thou talk'st of nothing" (1, 4, 101–2). Even Mercutio understands as much about himself: "True, I talk of dreams, / Which are the children of an idle brain" (1, 4, 103–4). Beneath his charm is an emotional vacuum, and the thwarted passion that he has nowhere to bestow will lead to catastrophe.

Such emptiness is opposed to Romeo's capacity for desire, which overflows at the party after he sees Juliet: "O, she doth teach the torches to burn bright!" (1, 5, 51). Images of dark and light recur throughout the play, implying the disparity between the lovers and the world around them. We can also contrast the directness of Romeo's lines here with his earlier contorted declarations about Rosaline.

Almost at once a shadow is cast when Tybalt recognizes Romeo's voice and reports to Capulet (1, 5, 69–71). Juliet's father assuages Tybalt's eagerness to fight, but Tybalt's parting lines ensure that trouble will follow: "I will withdraw, but this intrusion shall, / Now seeming sweet, convert to bitt'rest gall" (1, 5, 102–3). Not even the immediate transition to the courtship of Juliet by Romeo eliminates the danger Tybalt poses.

The exchange that follows reaches the religious level of courtly love: "If I profane with my unworthiest hand / This holy shrine, the gentle sin is this" (1, 5, 104–5). The combination of fervor and elegant language allows us to believe that two people can fall in love so quickly. The two then engage in a gentle thrust and parry, as Juliet, younger yet somehow more experienced, guides Romeo, so even when he boldly kisses her, she counsels him, "You kiss by th' book" (1, 5, 122). But after the two learn about their identities, Juliet realizes her quandary: "My only love sprung from my only hate!" (1, 5, 152).

The Chorus sonnet that opens act 2 emphasizes the lovers' dilemma: "But passion lends them power, time means, to meet, / Temp'ring extremities with extreme sweet" (2, Prologue, 13–14). Romeo and Juliet will have hardly any time together. Thus we shall ask whether the love that sprouts so quickly between such young protagonists can be of sufficient depth to transcend its brevity and warrant the description "tragedy."

As Romeo heads for Juliet's home, he is pursued by Mercutio, who mocks the younger man's passion (2, 1, 36–44). Here again, much of Mercutio's language contains salacious humor, so tread carefully. More important to Romeo, however, is that Mercutio is ignorant about true love: "He jests at scars that never felt a wound" (2, 2, 1). Mercutio has a great deal of energy, but his only outlets are mockery, random sex, and violence.

We move next to the most celebrated lines of love in the English language. The images of the sun and moon are familiar, but the language is unaffected, and Romeo's passion dignifies it. Ironically, that same passion, uncontrolled by reason or practicality, will prove his downfall. At the moment, however, all that matters is his feeling. Even Juliet's merest sigh provokes response: "She speaks" (2, 2, 28). Nevertheless, something about Romeo is so overdone that in his own way he becomes comic.

Juliet, though, never loses perspective, as she explains in these celebrated lines: "O Romeo, Romeo, where art thou Romeo? / Deny thy father and refuse thy name" (2, 2, 36–37). Although she speaks to herself, she hopes that Romeo will not only literally alter his family name but also abandon the values of his family and expel the spirit of vengeance that encompasses them. Romeo, however, never articulates what she instinctively knows.

As Romeo gambols in the throes of romance, Juliet blends ardor with pertinent questions: "How camest thou hither, tell me, and wherefore?" (2, 2, 67). To which Romeo giddily replies, "With love's light wings did I o'erperch these walls" (2, 2, 71). Later she demands, "By whose direction found'st thou out this place?" (2, 2, 84), but Romeo again ignores practicalities: "By love, that first did prompt me to inquire" (2, 2, 85). Juliet also reminds him about the omnipresent threat from her family: "If they do see thee, they will murder thee" (2, 2, 75).

Juliet herself struggles between passion and restraint: "In truth, fair Montague, I am too fond, / And therefore thou mayst think my 'havior light" (2, 2, 103–4). Romeo, however, never weighs the ethical and emotional aspects of their crisis. For example, he swears by every convenient symbol: "Lady, by yonder blessèd moon I vow" (2, 2, 112), but Juliet sees deeper into his expression: "O, swear not by the moon, th' inconstant moon" (2, 4, 114). Like a chastened youngster, he asks for help: "What shall I swear by?" (2, 4, 117), so she soothes him: "Do not swear at all" (2, 4, 118).

Perhaps her most telling comment is how she envisions their existence together:

> I have no joy of this contract tonight.
> It is too rash, too unadvised, too sudden,
> Too like the lightening, which doth cease to be
> Ere one can say "It lightens." (2, 2, 124–27)

Images of explosion are frequently used to characterize their love, reflecting its fervor as well as its transience. She also adds:

> My bounty is as boundless as the sea,
> My love as deep. The more I give to thee,

> The more I have, for both are infinite. (2, 2, 140–42)

She will be as devoted as she says, but Romeo, in a moment that impels the tragedy, will not be so steadfast. Finally, after resisting several calls from the Nurse, Juliet offers her immortal farewell: "Good night, good night. Parting is such sweet sorrow" (2, 2, 199–200).

Scene 3 introduces us to Friar Lawrence, meditating over certain flowers and herbs that have both beneficial and dangerous qualities. His main thought, however, will resound: "Virtue itself turns vice, being misapplied, / And vice sometime by action dignified" (2, 3, 21–22). Good and bad, he reasons, are determined by circumstance and action. He also envisions conflicting elements within plants: "And where the worser is predominant, / Full soon the canker death eats up that plant" (2, 3, 30–31). At this moment Romeo enters, and we realize that the war the Friar has described is occurring within this young man.

On learning that Romeo has a new object of devotion, Friar Lawrence is astonished (2, 3, 69) but aware enough to issue a warning: "And art thou changed? Pronounce this sentence then: / Women may fall when there's no strength in men" (2, 3, 83–85). That prediction proves sadly true, but the Friar has one additional piece of advice: "Wisely and slow. They stumble that run fast" (2, 3, 101). The thought is not foolish, but it is impractical, for Romeo's nature is always to rush headlong.

We next see Mercutio and Benvolio bantering about Tybalt. Although they ridicule his quick temper, they acknowledge that he not a man to be trifled with (2, 4, 20–22). When Romeo joins them, they mock what they regard as his latest exercise in pointless and exaggerated yearning:

> For this driveling love is like a great
> natural that runs lolling up and down to hide his
> bauble in a hole. (2, 4, 93–95)

Such joshing reminds us of the real world in which Romeo and Juliet try to survive.

The entrance of the Nurse sparks more suggestive byplay, especially from Mercutio: "the bawdy hand of / the dial is now upon the prick of noon" (2, 4, 114–15). The Nurse feigns outrage but clearly enjoys being party to their "ropery" (2, 4, 148), even sharing it with her servant Peter. Eventually, however, she accepts Romeo's instructions for Juliet: "And there she shall at Friar Lawrence' cell / Be shrived and married" (2, 4, 185–86). The Nurse is another benign figure, but her flaws will prove hurtful. She also notes that *R* is the first letter of *Romeo* as well as *rosemary*, the flower of remembrance used at funerals and weddings.

As Juliet waits alone, her thoughts about the Nurse embody the tension between youth and age: "Had she affections and warm youthful blood, / She would be as swift in motion as a ball" (2, 5, 12–13). That contrast is at the core of the play. When the Nurse finally does arrive, she delays imparting information (2, 5, 40–48), almost to Juliet's breaking point: "Sweet, sweet, sweet nurse, tell me, what says my love?" (2, 5, 57–58).

The pace does not slow even with the Friar, whose wisdom will have painful repercussions: "These violent delights have violent ends / And their triumph die, like fire and power" (2, 6, 9–10). His advice is more misplaced: "Therefore love moderately. Long love doth so" (2, 6, 14). Unfortunately, Romeo and Juliet can proceed only according to the dictates of their character, all part of their fate.

From here the action moves fast. As Benvolio and Mercutio stroll on what is evidently a warm day, Mercutio's attitude suggests that what has been building for a while will soon explode:

> Thou—why, thou wilt quarrel with a man that hath
> a hair more or a hair less in his beard than
> thou hast. (3, 1, 18–20)

His accusation may be directed at Benvolio, but Mercutio is the one spoiling for a fight.

When a group of Capulets appears, led by Tybalt, the inevitable occurs, as Mercutio takes the phrase "my man" (3, 1, 57) as an excuse to brawl. Not even Romeo's protests (3, 1, 63–66) can prevent disaster, as Mercutio seizes the moment to begin a duel: "O calm, dishonorable, vile submission!" (3, 1, 74). The concept of honor, in Shakespeare almost always a feeble excuse for belligerence, suggests the vacuity of Mercutio's rancor. Romeo tries to intervene, but in the hubbub Mercutio is fatally wounded.

As he lies in the street, whom does he blame? "A plague o' both your houses!" (3, 1, 111). Yet this accusation is unfair, because Mercutio instigated the fight. Even his joke about being a "grave man" (3, 1, 102) should not blind us to his responsibility and his wasted, destructive life. Romeo's response is that of a man who acts without thought:

> O sweet Juliet,
> Thy beauty hath made me effeminate
> And in my temper softened valor's steel. (3, 1, 118–20)

At first his desire to avenge his friend's death may seem admirable, but in fact Romeo has yielded to the worst values of his society: He equates manhood with the capacity to kill.

Imbued with intent to avenge in the name of honor, Romeo fails to anticipate consequences (3, 1, 130–34), and once again rashness overwhelms him. After he slays Tybalt, and Benvolio warns him to escape (3, 1, 138–41), Romeo can only confess pathetically, "O, I am Fortune's fool!" (3, 1, 142). The line is vital. Romeo tries to avoid responsibility, but he has been a traitor to the idealized love to which he aspired and thereby doomed any hope of a life with Juliet.

Consider the overall predicament. Here is a character sensitive enough to fall in love but vulnerable to forces of tradition. He is emotional but out of control. In other words, his best attributes undo him, and thus he faces the dilemma endemic to the Shakespearean tragic hero. Still, because the slaying of Tybalt is instantaneous rather than deeply considered, it lacks the resonance of more profound reactions by later figures.

As a crowd gathers, Benvolio tries to remove blame from Romeo by ignoring Mercutio's actions in precipitating the violence (3, 1, 172–78). The Capulets then demand Romeo's life, but the Prince modifies his edict of the first scene: "Immediately we do exile him hence" (3, 1, 197). True culpability, however, is established later, after Juliet waits alone and in her soliloquy longs for both spiritual and physical union with Romeo (3, 2, 10–13). She then ruminates on her predicament: "Give me my Romeo, and when I shall die, / Take him and cut him out in little stars" (3, 2, 23–24). Thus she establishes a recurring motif: the link between love and death.

When the Nurse arrives, she again delays communicating vital information. After she reveals the truth about Romeo's slaying of Tybalt, Juliet's initial reaction is powerful:

> O nature, what hadst thou to do in hell
> When thou didst bower the spirit of a fiend
> In mortal paradise of such sweet flesh? (3, 2, 86–88)

To which "fiend" does she refer? The spirit of revenge? Or of Mercutio? Although she will vacillate from so absolute a verdict after the Nurse speaks badly of Romeo, Juliet initially blames him. She thereby becomes the chief ethical presence in the play, and her judgment is the one we respect.

Seeking refuge in the Friar's cell, Romeo repeats the word *banishèd* again and again, then accuses the Friar of failing to be sympathetic: "Thou canst not speak of that thou dost not feel" (3, 3, 67). Yet the more Romeo raves, the more he sounds like a boy throwing a tantrum. Then the Nurse reports on Juliet's desolation, urging Romeo: "Stand an you be a man" (3, 3, 96), a line the Friar will echo: "Art thou a man?" (3, 3, 119). Ironically, Romeo slew Tybalt to establish Romeo's own manhood, but now that quality is questioned.

The Friar, however, is not finished. After Romeo in characteristically headlong fashion threatens to kill himself, the Friar takes him to task:

> Why railest thou on thy birth, the heaven, and earth,
> Since birth and heaven and earth all three do meet
> In thee at once, which thou at once wouldst lose? (3, 3, 129–31)

Like all human beings, the Friar says, Romeo is a product of his world. Nevertheless, he controls his destiny and owes both Juliet and himself proper action. Versions of that sentiment resound through Shakespeare's plays. At this juncture Romeo gathers himself, accepts a ring from the Nurse, and leaves to join Juliet.

Before they can reunite, however, we have a bizarre interlude, as Capulet and Lady Capulet resolve that, despite Tybalt's death, Juliet must still marry Paris. The only concession the parents will make is that to prevent the impression of indifference, the wedding party will be limited to "some half a dozen friends" (3, 4, 30). Were the suggestion not callous, it might be comic.

When Romeo and Juliet awaken the next morning, they seem to have exchanged priorities, as Juliet becomes the more romantic, denying the song of the lark, while Romeo responds that morning has come (3, 5, 1–11). But once she acknowledges the truth, Juliet insists that Romeo must hurry away to save himself (3, 5, 26–30). More importantly, she maintains the foreshadowing of doom that has always haunted this relationship:

> O God, I have an ill-divining soul!
> Methinks I see thee, now thou art so low,
> As one dead in the bottom of a tomb. (3, 5, 54–56)

Again we are reminded that Juliet is the wiser of the two.

When she is by herself, we also remember that she is alone in the world. While her parents assume that her unhappiness is caused by the loss of Tybalt, we understand that she mourns Romeo: "Indeed, I shall never be satisfied / With Romeo till I behold him—dead" (3, 5, 98–99). In her isolation, she seems like any young person who cannot confess true feelings to members of the older generation, and that characteristic is part of what gives this play its appeal: It dramatizes not just love but young love.

To herself Juliet prays for Romeo, but to her parents she must feign other emotions. Thus the mix of bitterness and wit in her language:

> I pray you, tell my lord and father, madam,
> I will not marry yet, and when I do I swear
> It shall be Romeo, whom you know I hate,
> Rather than Paris. (3, 5, 125–28)

She is already married but remains true to her own feelings while denying her parents' order. This condition is especially painful when Capulet insists that she marry Paris:

> Hang thee, young baggage, disobedient wretch!
> I tell thee what: get thee to church o' Thursday
> Or never after look me in the face. (3, 5, 166–68)

Until this scene, his paternal authoritarianism has been disguised. Now it emerges in all its harshness. In retrospect, we shall also see this line as ironic, given that Juliet's death is imminent.

Even the Nurse proves an unsatisfactory confidante. Speaking of Paris, she says, "O, he's a lovely gentleman! / Romeo's a dishclout to him" (3, 5,

231–32). Her lack of feeling, again meant kindly, leaves Juliet furious: "Ancient damnation, O most wicked fiend!" (3, 5, 248). She has no choice but to escape to the Friar's cell, where she hopes to find salvation: "If all else fail, myself have power to die" (3, 5, 255). Unlike Romeo, Juliet remains in control of her mind and heart.

Her first task is disposing of Paris, who still courts her, although because of his ignorance of what has transpired, his attempts arouse in us sympathy tinged with irony. After Juliet ushers him out, she confesses to the Friar that she is prepared to take her life (4, 1, 51–68), but he has conceived a plan by which she drinks from a vial of liquid that will give her the appearance of death. The Friar will forward this plan to Romeo, but even before we learn the outcome, this scheme appears convoluted and vulnerable to circumstance, a perfect reflection of the Friar's character.

In scene 2, wedding plans move quickly, as Capulet's relief strikes us as both infuriating and blind: "My heart if wondrous light / Since this same wayward girl is so reclaimed" (4, 2, 48–49). Almost immediately, Juliet dismisses the Nurse, afraid to confide in her: "My dismal scene I needs must act alone" (4, 3, 20). In retrospect, willingness to confide in someone might have prevented Juliet's death, but her independence has always been her strength which, as befits the protagonist in a tragedy, also leads to her downfall.

Left by herself, Juliet is beset by nightmarish visions. She imagines that the Friar might betray her (4, 3, 25–28), then pictures herself lying beside dead Tybalt in the vault. At last, driven almost mad by fear, she downs the contents of the vial. Whatever suspense we might feel builds during further marriage preparations, but when the sleeping Juliet is discovered, our feelings are again divided. We feel compassion for the Nurse and Lady Capulet, and even Capulet himself seems stricken with unbearable grief. Yet none of them is completely innocent.

Two lines undercut the moment. First, Friar Lawrence tries to soothe the company: "She's not well married that lives married long, / But she's best married that dies married young" (4, 5, 83–84). The sentiment would ring false at any time, but that the Friar knows the truth makes him a hypocrite. The second is from Capulet: "All things that we ordainèd festival / Turn from their office to black funeral" (4, 5, 90–91). The response befits a man who puts his own convenience first. Earlier he stopped Tybalt from interrupting the party (1, 5, 80–83) and tried to force Juliet to marry Paris (3, 5, 158–62). Now he smooths over his daughter's death.

Throughout these scenes, the audience's range of emotions is remarkable. We know that Juliet is still alive, but we see the pain her masquerade has caused, even if it is expressed poorly and even if we do not approve of the people who suffer. We also know that the ending of this play will be tragic, so our own feelings are confused. Sadness, irony, perhaps bitter laughter: Shakespeare twists us in many directions.

In act 5, Romeo experiences nightmares of his own, again uniting images of love and death (5, 1, 1–12). When Balthasar brings word that he believes Juliet has actually died, Romeo is determined to act: "Then I deny you, stars!" (5, 1, 25). Without waiting for news from the friar, Romeo races to Juliet. Once again he acts impulsively, and once again results will be calamitous.

His first stop is the apothecary, who is reluctant to sell Romeo poisonous drugs, but at last Romeo acts independently from society's rules and urges the apothecary to do likewise: "The world is not thy friend, nor the world's law" (5, 1, 76). Scene 2 then explains why the friar's missive failed to reach Romeo: "the infectious pestilence did reign" (5, 2, 10). Should we interpret this as fate? No, because the friar's plan invited disruption, and as such it is one more example of human misjudgment.

As the final scene unfolds, Paris mourns Juliet. Although he is not dislikeable, he competes for our affection against Romeo, and thus no matter how ardently Paris speaks, he must be the object of our antipathy. When Romeo enters and attempts to pry open Juliet's tomb, he speaks of the "womb of death" (5, 3, 45), one more welding of images of love and death. Inevitably, it seems, Paris challenges Romeo, the two fight, and Paris is killed. Only then does Romeo recognize him as Mercutio's kinsman.

As Romeo looks at Juliet's body, he notices her appearance: "Beauty's ensign yet / Is crimson in thy lips and in thy cheeks" (5, 3, 94–95). Common sense would suggest that she may not be dead, and the detail is an effective insertion by Shakespeare to raise our hopes. Then, seconds before he drinks the poison, Romeo invokes an intriguing image: "Thou desperate pilot" (5, 3, 117). Earlier at her balcony, he said of himself, "I am no pilot" (2, 2, 87). There he was a brazen but uncertain lover. Now he is a man battered by life. Still, as usual, Romeo does not think and instead hurries to drinks the poison: "Thus with a kiss I die" (5, 3, 120).

Friar Lawrence arrives, appropriately late, and when Juliet awakens and sees what has occurred, he offers to help her escape and live: "Among a sisterhood of holy nuns" (5, 3, 162). That he could even propose such an idea shows how out of touch he is. He even protests: "Come, go, good Juliet. I dare no longer stay" (5, 3, 164). We sense his moral cowardice, his fear of standing up for what it is he has done. In a moment that borders on comedy even under these circumstances, Juliet urges him: "Go get thee hence, for I will not away" (5, 3, 165). After the Friar slips away, Juliet stabs herself; her devotion remains as absolute as she promised.

After word of the two deaths spreads, the families arrive. To our relief, the Friar finds the courage to return and, with assistance from Balthasar and the page, relates the events that led to this moment. In response, Capulet makes a gesture of reconciliation: "This is my daughter's jointure, for no more / Can I demand" (5, 3, 307–8). Montague, though, seems to take the offer as a challenge: "But I can give thee more, / For I will ray her statue in pure gold" (5, 3, 309–10). Does the rivalry between the two families still flicker?

In considering *Romeo and Juliet* as part of Shakespeare's tragedies, we note that the play lacks a central tragic figure. Perhaps the title characters are too young and without the necessary stature. In other words, neither has sufficiently far to fall. Moreover, neither has tragic complexity. Until the very end, Juliet is largely reactive, while even before he kills Tybalt, Romeo does not undergo an inner struggle. He never clarifies or even seems to grasp how he is torn between Juliet and his family.

Yet one quality lifts this play to the realm of the tragic: the sense of irrevocable loss. Romeo and Juliet intuit that their love soars over all that surrounds them, and they are unwilling to live without that love. That devotion is their greatness, and its destruction makes the play tragic.

Chapter Two

Julius Caesar

One effective way to begin discussing this play is with a simple question: Who is the main character? Some students will answer Brutus, who undergoes the crucial ethical quandary. Others will say Cassius, the prime mover of the conspiracy. Others will answer Antony, who turns the conspiracy back on its instigators. And still others will answer Caesar himself, who towers over the rest and even in death holds away.

But this play has a fifth major character, one too often neglected. It is the most powerful of all and the one the other major characters fear. This character is the reason the principals act, speak, and, most of all, think the way they do. This character is the Roman citizenry, more accurately regarded as the "mob." True, Rome is not a democratic state. Its leaders, however, operate under the assumption that whoever hopes to lead the city must have the support of the great mass of people. That perspective turns the play into a portrait of political maneuvering, exactly how students should regard it and with an eye toward contemporary parallels.

Of Shakespeare's ten tragedies, four are set in ancient Rome: *Titus Andronicus*, *Julius Caesar*, *Antony and Cleopatra*, and *Coriolanus*. All, but especially *Julius Caesar* and *Coriolanus*, touch on issues raised in Shakespeare's two tetralogies based on internal and external conflicts in English history of the fifteenth century, and thus these Roman plays, too, may be interpreted as revealing Shakespeare's vision of political life.

Before examining the text, you should provide some historical background. In 60 BCE, Caesar was a member of the ruling triumvirate of Rome, along with Pompey and Crassus. In 53 BCE, Crassus died in battle, and in 49 BCE, in an attempt to gain absolute authority, Caesar flouted the Roman Senate by leading his forces across the Rubicon River in Northern Italy and against the armies of Pompey. In 47 BCE, Caesar defeated Pompey, then pursued him to Egypt, where Pompey was killed and Caesar enjoyed a dalliance with Cleopatra. Civil war continued for two more years, until Caesar returned to Rome, where with the support of the populace he ruled until his assassination in 44 BCE.

Shakespeare's primary source for this play is Plutarch's *Lives of the Noble Grecians and Romans*, but he shapes facts for his own purposes, as events that historically covered several years are encapsulated into six days. Shakespeare also acknowledges Caesar's physical defects (to be mentioned later) but omits incidents that would portray him as far more dictatorial. In the play he is arrogant but clearly a great man, feared and respected by virtually all.

Political unrest is established in the first scene, as the mob wanders aimlessly, mocking tribunes Flavius and Marullus, until the latter berates them:

> You blocks, you stones, you worse than senseless
>   things!
> O you hard hearts, you cruel men of Rome,
> Knew you not Pompey? (1, 1, 39–42)

The appeal to past glories would not be out of place at a major party convention. But as if to assuage the masses after Marullus's harangue, Flavius offers another aspect of political oratory, the soothing benediction: "Go, go, good countrymen, and for this fault / Assemble all the poor men of your sort" (1, 1, 61–62).

One implication of both these addresses is that the mob's enthusiasm for Caesar gave him the power he currently wields. Another is that the man who can appropriate that power will rule Rome. After the crowd disperses, however, Flavius's kind manner changes into cynicism: "See whe'er their basest mettle be not moved" (1, 1, 66). He insinuates that those he calls the "vulgar" (1, 1, 75) are mindless and therefore malleable. The two tribunes then set about desecrating statues of Caesar, reflecting more widespread dissatisfaction with his rule.

This scene contains dialogue patterns that recur throughout the play. Speakers constantly rouse listeners, then cajole and flatter them, and then comment derisively. Nearly every significant speech in the play, whether private or public, is firebrand oratory filled with allusion and accusation, all intended to persuade. Yet such demagogic tactics become self-destructive, for they force speakers to cultivate hypocrisy. The result is that individual existences, close friendships, and eventually an entire society are left in rubble.

In 1, 2, we catch a brief glimpse of Caesar. His one-word summoning of his wife, Calphurnia, suggests that he expects obeisance, while his instruction to Antony to touch her during the race indicates that he is superstitious. Meanwhile his dismissal of the soothsayer who warns about the Ides of

March shows Caesar's need to demonstrate confidence. All these qualities make him vulnerable to flattery that will result in his downfall.

After Caesar and his party leave, we meet Brutus, whose demeanor ensures that we care about him. He ponders matters deeply and will soon evince a social conscience and a reassuring lack of ambition. Yet he also regards himself as seriously as others do:

> Vexèd I am
> Of late with passions of some difference,
> Conceptions only proper to myself. (1, 2, 45–47)

He oozes profundity and even declares that he should not be expected to observe niceties that other men follow (1, 2, 53). Such vanity is susceptible to manipulation, as Cassius is about to demonstrate.

His goal is to convince Brutus to act against Caesar. First Cassius uses flattery (1, 2, 64–68), then resorts to false modesty (1, 2, 74–76). After an offstage shout conveniently intrudes, Brutus casually mentions: "I do fear the people / Choose Caesar for their king" (1, 2, 85–86). Cassius shrewdly seizes on "fear," inviting Brutus to establish himself as a moral exemplar, and Brutus obliges with this key line: "For let the gods so speed me as I love / The name of honor more than I fear death" (1, 2, 95–96). The use of *honor* alerts us that Brutus's primary concern is his reputation.

Cassius certainly knows as much: "Well, honor is the subject of my story" (1, 2, 99), and he launches into a diatribe on Caesar's lack of fitness for office. He dramatizes Caesar's physical weakness while swimming (1, 2, 107–18), then follows with a reference to Caesar's epilepsy (1, 2, 126–35). The implication is that a man with such deficiencies lacks sufficient masculine qualities and thus the prerogative to rule.

Cassius moves next to the glorification of Brutus: "The fault, dear Brutus, is not in our stars, / But in ourselves, that we are underlings" (1, 2, 147–48). Yet Cassius knows that Brutus is not susceptible to promises of authority and thus dwells on Rome's history, now besmirched by Caesar: "Age, thou art shamed! / Rome, thou hast lost the breed of noble bloods!" (1, 2, 159–60). Like Marullus in scene 1, Cassius tries to rouse his audience to action.

Brutus's response is muted:

> What you have said
> I will consider; what you have to say
> I will with patience hear, and find a time
> Both meet to hear and answer such high things. (1, 2, 176–79)

He sounds as if he is trying to conceive some way to sanction an action that he knows is immoral. In the meantime, as Cassius plays Brutus's humble confidante, periodic shouts from the offstage mob, like cries from a primitive horde, remind the two men where real power in Rome lies.

When Caesar and his entourage return, Calphurnia and Cicero look distressed, hinting that Caesar may have had a spell. Caesar's own remarks, though, are more telling: "Yond Cassius has a lean and hungry look / He thinks too much. Such men are dangerous" (1, 2, 204–5). The insight into Cassius is accurate, but Brutus, too, thinks too much. The danger he poses, however, is more subtle. Nonetheless, Caesar's pride prevents him from taking care: "I rather tell thee what is to be feared / Than what I fear, for always I am Caesar" (1, 2, 221–22). The deafness mentioned in the next line, by the way, is Shakespeare's invention.

Casca's derisive report on Caesar's refusal to accept the crown sounds like the testimony of a world-weary reporter: "if Caesar had stabbed their mothers, they would have done no less" (1, 2, 285–86). We recognize Caesar's own performance as the work of a master manipulator of the public. Casca also adds one more piece of news: "Marullus and Flavius, for pulling scarves off Caesar's images, are put to silence" (1, 2, 296–97). Does this abuse add further justification for the overthrow of Caesar? Or is Cassius's scheme still the product of a man jealous of power?

When Brutus departs, Cassius muses on what he has accomplished:

> Well, Brutus, thou art noble. Yet I see
> Thy honorable mettle may be wrought
> From that it is disposed. (1, 2, 320–22)

The use of *honorable* alerts us to Cassius's confidence that Brutus may be controlled, and *mettle* recalls Flavius's comment about the mob (1, 1, 66). Had we any doubt that political chicanery is at work, these lines confirm that impression. So does Cassius's plan to throw into Brutus's house several messages, ostensibly from other Romans. Cassius understands that when an individual like Brutus is flattered, his pride will take over.

Next we see Cicero and Casca, now fearful because of the storm:

> Either there is civil strife in heaven,
> Or else the world, too saucy with the gods,
> Incenses them to send destruction. (1, 3, 11–13)

The potential turmoil in Rome resounds through the heavens, a manifestation of how events in the microcosm influence the macrocosm. Casca then relates other unnatural phenomena that have left him shaken (1, 3, 15–32), but later Cassius dismisses them as "instruments of fear and warning / Unto some monstrous state" (1, 3, 73–74). He is instead scornful of the mob: "What trash is Rome, / What rubbish, and what offal" (1, 3, 112–13), and clarifies Brutus's inclinations: "Three parts of him / Is ours already" (1, 3, 159–60). Casca agrees (1, 3, 162–65) and hopes that Brutus's reputation for integrity will legitimize what the three know is an illegitimate act.

Meanwhile Brutus undergoes a struggle of his own: "It must be by his death. And for my part / I know no personal cause to spurn at him" (2, 1,

10–11). He is caught between doing right by Rome and committing an unjustified murder. Does his supposition that Caesar might be corrupted justify that murder? His fears take the form of terrifying dreams (2, 1, 64–72), a sign that his conscience is pained. He admits, too, that he has not slept since his earlier conversation with Cassius, and his inner disorder mirrors the disorder in Rome. Trying to do right by everybody, Brutus ends up pleasing no one.

The entrance of the rest of the conspirators, who look and act like thugs, further perturbs Brutus, who wishes they could plan in the open (2, 1, 84–93). He also decries the necessity for an oath (2, 1, 125–51), and his rambling address suggests that he is trying to convince himself as much as the others. Indeed, he tries to avoid any action that would taint the purity of their enterprise. Is he serious and noble or foolish and impractical? How we regard his character goes a long way toward determining how we regard the play as a whole.

Brutus also makes tactical blunders. He disdains the cooperation of Cicero, who might furnish additional prestige but might also be a rival for leadership (2, 1, 162–64). And when Cassius calls for Antony to be killed as well, Brutus rejects that proposal: "Let's be sacrificers, but not butchers, Caius" (2, 1, 179). Brutus's intention is to have an assassination without blood, a noble slaughter: "We shall be called purgers, not murderers" (2, 1, 193). Cassius, ever the realist, remains unconvinced: "Yet I fear him" (2, 1, 197), but is helpless to alter the judgment of the man who lends legitimacy to their cause.

At the anachronistic chiming of the clock, Cassius asks how Caesar may be persuaded to go to the Capitol, but Decius reassures everyone that he knows how to flatter Caesar: "For I can give his humor the true bent, / And I will bring him to the Capitol" (2, 1, 227–28). The same description could apply to Brutus, also vulnerable to toadying by subordinates. No wonder he can gauge Caesar's moods. Here Brutus attempts to salvage dignity from this scheme: "Good gentlemen, look fresh and merrily" (2, 1, 243). He cannot accept the reality of the crime he is about to perpetrate.

Perhaps the saddest aspect of Brutus's charade is his treatment of Portia. He clearly loves her, even as she perceives the truth:

> You have some sick offense within your mind,
> Which by the right and virtue of my place
> I ought to know of. (2, 1, 288–90)

Then she kneels. He lifts her but is still ashamed to admit his plans, a sure sign that he knows that they are misguided. We recognize that the disparity between his public role and his private intentions has created a schism within him that he is unable to fuse. Whatever we feel about his political performance, we understand his agonies as a husband: "O you gods, / Render me worthy of this noble wife!" (2, 1, 326–27).

Thus Brutus's dilemma is unique among Shakespeare's tragic heroes. True, like Hamlet he is a man of thought placed in a situation where he must be a man of action, and like Hamlet he must battle within himself over whether to pursue a particular course. But only Brutus must publicly advocate that course and thereby convince everyone else of what he himself does not believe. As a result, he is reduced to an ineffective rhetorician.

That evening, when Caesar hears about Calphurnia's dreams that are filled with bad omens (2, 2, 13–26), he belittles them: "Cowards die many times before their deaths; / The valiant never taste of death but once" (2, 2, 34–35). The sentiment is noble but also haughty, as if Caesar is inviting trouble, as he does in a later line: "Danger knows full well / That Caesar is more dangerous than he" (2, 2, 47–48). Nonetheless, to satisfy Calphurnia, he agrees to remain at home.

All that is needed to make Caesar change his mind are clever words from Decius, who reinterprets Calphurnia's dream:

> Your statue spouting blood in many pipes,
> In which so many smiling Romans bathed,
> Signifies that from you great Rome shall suck
> Reviving blood. (2, 2, 90–93)

This explanation sounds feeble, but Decius offers one clinching bit of explanation. Speaking of the Roman citizenry, he says: "If Caesar hide himself, shall they not whisper / 'Lo, Caesar is afraid?'" (2, 2, 105–6). Even the possibility of mockery from the mob unnerves Caesar, who understands that command must be constantly reinforced.

In 2, 3, Artemidorus reads his warning to Caesar. Although we know what happened historically, this interlude creates a bit of suspense. The actual number of conspirators against Caesar was roughly sixty, and Artemidorus was an associate of several of them. Thus this scene, in combination with Portia's inquiries in the next, provide a moment's pause before the inevitable assassination.

At the forum, Caesar continues his arrogant behavior. He dismisses the soothsayer, then Artemidorus: "What touches us ourself shall be last served" (3, 1, 8). Metellus Cimber, pleading for his banished brother, receives even more discourteous treatment: "If thou dost bend and pray and fawn for him, / I spurn thee like a cur out of my way" (3, 1, 50–51). And as the conspirators gather around him:

> But I am constant as the Northern Star,
> Of whose true fixed and resting quality
> There is no fellow in the firmament. (3, 1, 66–68)

With each line, he further invites retribution.

Consider, however, the overall portrait of Caesar. He is proud, and his treatment of subordinates and even his wife is cavalier. Yet his leadership and accomplishments are never questioned. Do his flaws, then, justify his murder? In light of the insurrection unleashed after the act, the answer must be no.

Deep down, Brutus recognizes this fact. Thus after the ferocious stabbing, with the bloody corpse of Caesar lying before him and "*Et tu, Brutè?*" (3, 1, 85) still resounding, Brutus attempts to play diplomat: "So are we Caesar's friends, that have abridged / His time of fearing death" (3, 1, 116–17). The thought is nonsense, as is his intention to walk through the marketplace: "Let's all cry 'Peace, freedom, and liberty!'" (3, 1, 122).

When a servant enters to beg for Antony's safe entrance, Brutus remains blindly idealistic: "He shall be satisfied, and by my honor, / Depart untouched" (3, 1, 156–57). With each use of *honor*, the word sounds more vacuous. As Antony mourns over Caesar, Brutus is so desperate to alleviate tensions that he rationalizes to the point of absurdity: "Our hearts you see not; they are pitiful" (3, 1, 185). Cassius, however, characteristically offers Antony something more practical: "Your voice shall be as strong as any man's / In the disposing of new dignities" (3, 1, 193–94). Meanwhile Brutus remains preoccupied with speaking to the crowd and ensuring that his actions are judged in the best light (3, 1, 195–99).

Antony, however, will have none of it and continues to brood over Caesar's death, even as he says he seeks "reasons / Why and wherein Caesar was dangerous" (3, 1, 242–43). Brutus fails to see Antony's irony: "Or else were this a savage spectacle" (3, 1, 244). He even repeats *reasons*, as if the assassination could be so directly explained. Brutus's final blunders are, first, permitting Antony to speak at Caesar's funeral and, second, allowing Antony to speak last. Cassius, ever the realist, is dubious (3, 1, 255–59), but Brutus remains impervious to explanation.

Here is a moment to ask the class which strategy makes for an effective political address: appeal to reason or appeal to emotion. Ask, too, which position on the program is preferable: first or last. Brutus is determined to maintain the moral high ground but, in doing so reveals that he lacks the determination necessary for political infighting. When the power of the mob is the ultimate weapon, civility is a luxury. To clarify such a viewpoint, you might ask for examples from recent political speeches.

Left alone, Antony releases the fury that has built up inside him: "O pardon me, thou bleeding piece of earth, / That I am meek and gentle with these butchers" (3, 1, 280–81). We remember that Brutus was desperate that the conspirators not be regarded as "butchers" (2, 1, 179). Moreover, Antony's willingness to unleash Ate, the god of discord (3, 1, 297), and "let slip the dogs of war" (3, 1, 299) confirms our suspicion that Brutus has misread Antony's intentions. True, Antony's ruthlessness sets off Brutus's moral rectitude, but events that follow suggest that, in politics, pragmatism triumphs.

A brilliant performance by Antony in 3, 2, made even greater by its contrast with Brutus's lackluster effort, is spectacular. Even before Brutus speaks, however, the second Plebeian wants to hear "reasons" (3, 2, 10), a laughable claim. We also see that Brutus's speech is in prose, suggesting its lifelessness. What is the essence of Brutus's words: "But, as he was ambitious, I slew him" (3, 2, 28)? Which politician is not ambitious? Brutus's subsequent call for objections from the mob is phony, for who can speak out after Brutus essentially brands any opposition as treasonous?

The sight of Antony entering with the corpse is bound to arouse compassion from even enemies of Caesar. Brutus, however, cannot deal with political reality and prepares to leave. Before he does, though, the crowd's reactions to him are telling. "Let him be Caesar" (3, 2, 53), shouts the third Plebeian. "Caesar's better parts / Shall be crowned in Brutus" (3, 2, 54–55) adds the fourth. Shakespeare's implication is clear: The people want a dictator. Despite Brutus's vision, they want to be told what to do and what to think.

Antony's speech is everything Brutus's is not. He consistently invokes *honor* and *honorable*, playing on Brutus's use of the words. He recalls Caesar's triumphs, differentiating them from the petty lives of his murderers. He pretends that Caesar's rejection of the crown was other than political theater (3, 2, 104–6). Even his reference to "brutish beasts" (3, 2, 114), with the subliminal pun on *Brutus*, implies the cruelty of the assassins. At this juncture, Antony turns away in apparent tears, to which the first Plebeian comments, "Methinks there is much reason in his sayings" (3, 2, 118). Exactly the opposite is true.

The gambit with the will drives the crowd into a frenzy. Antony pledges to reveal the contents but always withdraws that promise because: "It is not meet you know how Caesar loved you. / You are not wood, you are not stone, but men" (3, 2, 153–54). The images recall Marullus's words at 1, 1, 40. After Antony sends the mob running off, then back, he pulls out what he claims is the will. But is it? We have no way of knowing.

Antony's most brilliant stroke is his use of Caesar's cloak, supposedly worn: "That day he overcame the Nervii" (3, 2, 185). Then Antony graphically re-creates where every stab tore into that cloak, but how can he know which is which, including the one supposedly inflicted by Brutus, "the most unkindest cut of all" (3, 2, 195)? Reality doesn't matter. Emotions take over the mob, as they feel every blow of the knife personally, and Caesar's wounds become their own. Finally Antony reads what he claims are the terms of Caesar's will, but again we have no guarantee that what he pronounces is accurate.

If opportunity permits, show the class the first two scenes of act 3 from the 1953 film version of *Julius Caesar*. The stars are Marlon Brando, James Mason, and Sir John Gielgud, and all sorts of directorial and performance touches will give the group much to appreciate and discuss. Our overall impression of the scene, both on the page and on the screen, is that Antony is brilliant but calculating: "Mischief, thou art afoot; / Take thou what course thou wilt" (3, 2, 275–76). The crowd is loathsome.

The funeral oration is generally regarded as the climax of the play, but the short scene that follows is the dramatic high point, a portrait of mob power run amok. Even when the people realize that the man they have captured is not Cinna the conspirator but Cinna the poet, they kill him anyway. In the words of the fourth Plebeian: "It is no matter. His name's Cinna" (3, 3, 34). Our final glimpse of the mob is of them running the streets, in Antony's words, like the "dogs of war" (3, 1, 299). Their mindless energy suggests the need for an authoritarian government to control them.

In acts 4 and 5, this play loses some vitality. Brutus, Cassius, Antony, and the rest are primarily politicians, and thus are less interesting as military leaders. Still, their essential natures pierce through. Antony, for instance, dismisses his colleague Lepidus in cold terms: "This is a slight, unmeritable man, / Meet to be sent on errands" (4, 1, 14–15). Octavius tries to defend him: "But he's a tried and valiant soldier" (4, 1, 32). Antony, though, is interested only in utility: "So is my horse, Octavius" (4, 1, 33).

Brutus's attitude, too, remains the same, as he shows in scenes 2 and 3. Initially, with Lucilius, he seems resigned to Cassius's failings (4, 2, 25–30) but then accuses Cassius personally of having an:

> itching palm,
> To sell and mart your offices for gold
> To undeservers. (4, 3, 10–12)

An outraged Cassius denies the allegations, and the two are soon reduced to petty bickering about who called whom a better soldier (4, 3, 61–62). Brutus's recourse is to retreat behind a high-minded posture:

> There is no terror, Cassius, in your threats,
> For I am armed so strong in honesty
> That they pass by me as the idle wind,
> Which I respect not. (4, 3, 75–78)

His tone sounds like that of Caesar in earlier scenes.

Cassius protests once more: "A friend should bear his friend's infirmities, / But Brutus makes mine greater than they are" (4, 3, 96–97). Even so, Brutus tries to remain above the fray: "I do not, till you practice them on me" (4, 3, 98). In fact, Cassius has practiced them on Brutus, flattering and cajoling him into the conspiracy, but Brutus was blind. Does he refuse to acknowledge baser desires, or is he simply out of touch with ordinary feeling?

Brutus reports Portia's death in a strangely impassive tone, so much so that Cassius seems more moved: "How 'scaped I killing when I crossed you so?" (4, 3, 171). Moments later, when the report is confirmed, Brutus dismisses such talk (4, 3, 183–84). Does he wish to eliminate all distractions? Or is he too pained by the unhappiness he brought on her? He seems unequally unmoved by word that a hundred senators have been executed. Once more the horror of reality looms.

The next argument between Brutus and Cassius again reflects their personalities. Cassius believes with good reason that luring the enemy to march toward the troops of Brutus and Cassius will wear out opposing forces (4, 3, 229–32), while Brutus insists that their own troops should march to end up between opposing armies. His rationale is more idealistic: "Our legions are brim full, our cause is ripe" (4, 3, 246). As usual, Brutus cannot imagine that his nobility will permit defeat and insists on seizing what he believes is the proper moment: "There is a tide in the affairs of men / Which, taken at the flood, leads on to fortune" (4, 3, 249–50).

Moments later, the Ghost of Caesar appears before Brutus, proclaiming itself: "Thy evil spirit" (4, 3, 325). Elizabethans of all classes believed in the existence of ghosts, which generally took one of two forms. Objective ghosts, such as the one that stands before Hamlet and his associates, were visible to several people and therefore presumed to be actually present. Subjective ghosts, such as Caesar's here, are figments of one individual's imagination, and thus we may assume that this vision is a manifestation of Brutus's conscience, warning of his forthcoming death at Philippi (4, 3, 330).

Act 5 uses a technique familiar from other plays of Shakespeare: dramatizing war as a series of short, quick exchanges. First Octavius and Antony disagree on strategy. The key comment is from Octavius: "I do not cross you, but I will do so" (5, 1, 21). He anticipates the greater conflict that will be at the heart of Shakespeare's *Antony and Cleopatra*, written ten years after this play.

The four leaders then meet in a ritual more familiar to medieval warfare than conflict from this period. The men exchange insults and challenges, but after all the braggadocio, one remark from Cassius to Brutus stands out: "If we do lose this battle, then is this / The very last time we shall speak together" (5, 1, 107–8). His swagger has disappeared. Cassius seems prepared to commit suicide rather than suffer the indignity of capture, but Brutus, head ever high, cannot conceive of being treated that way. Of himself he says, "He bears too great a mind" (5, 1, 123).

In 5, 3, confusion reigns, as Titinius reports that Brutus advanced his forces too quickly. Cassius flees for safety and in the confusion kills himself with the sword that he used to kill Caesar (5, 3, 50–51). Then word comes that Brutus has actually surrounded Octavius's army. The conflicting bulletins are almost comic, but more important is that these politicians are unsuited for warfare. One line from Messala sums up the situation: "Mistrust of good success hath done this deed" (5, 3, 74).

When Brutus comes across Cassius's body, he knows where to lay blame: "O Julius Caesar, thou art mighty yet" (5, 3, 105). Nonetheless, when Brutus realizes the battle is lost, he reverts to his customary self: "My heart doth joy that yet in all my life / I found no man but he was true to me" (5, 5, 38–39). How little he has learned, for people have deceived him repeatedly. We sense that had he the opportunity to do everything again, he would proceed the same way.

He adds one more ironic reflection:

> I shall have glory by this losing day
> More than Octavius and Mark Antony
> By this vile conquest shall attain unto. (5, 5, 40–42)

Not only does Brutus continue to reach for honor, but also his prediction is wrong because he and Cassius have been judged among the most notorious traitors in history. Indeed, one measure of their ignominy is that in Dante's *Inferno* they are condemned, along with Judas Iscariot, to the ninth and innermost circle of hell, where each is chewed and tortured in a mouth of Satan.

Antony ends by giving Brutus a generous tribute: "This was the noblest Roman of them all" (5, 5, 74). He adds that only Brutus acted not out of envy, but for the good of Rome:

> His life was gentle and the elements
> So mixed in him that nature might stand up
> And say to the world "This was a man." (5, 5, 79–81)

Then we remember who is speaking: a superb politician. Does he mean what he says? Or is he pretending for the sake of expediency? Remember, too, that in this play the great mass of people is portrayed as fools and hypocrites. Does Antony mean that Brutus was the best to which humankind can aspire?

Octavius gives the final order: "Within my tent his bones tonight shall lie / Most like a soldier, ordered honorably" (5, 5, 84–85). Octavius probably does not use *honorably* ironically. Still, if ever a man did not warrant being buried like a soldier, that man is Brutus, who was forced into a role for which he was not suited. That dilemma anticipates the struggles of other tragic heroes in Shakespeare. We may admire Brutus or disapprove of him, but either way we understand that although his motives were generous, his own nature, in combination with circumstances determined by the world, ensured that he would be destroyed.

Chapter Three

Hamlet

One way to approach this play is to announce that outside of the Bible, it is the most influential work of literature ever written. It has been the subject of more critical writing than anyone can read, and the title character has received more analysis than any other fictional figure. Therefore the class's main goal during the days and weeks spent studying *Hamlet* should be to understand why it is so important.

Next, try to present an overall view of the play. Hamlet is a man confronted by a series of massive conflicts, inside and outside, and *Hamlet* dramatizes his attempts to solve those problems. From the very first line, the gripping "Who's there?" (1, 1, 1), the play concerns identity, and therefore Hamlet's dilemma is that of every human being: Given this time and these circumstances, how should he respond? What is his responsibility? Here is the reason that everyone who experiences this play identifies with the title character.

All of Shakespeare's tragic heroes suffer some version of this predicament, but Hamlet's is especially overwhelming. One reason is that his circumstances are never clear, either to him or to us. They constantly shift, like colors in a kaleidoscope, and from every perspective may be understood differently. At many moments, Hamlet tries to establish where he fits, but the values by which he judges his world make affirmation impossible.

Furthermore, not only does Hamlet react to his world, but also it reacts to him. He is a member of the royal family, and thus the health of the state rests to a significant degree on his physical and emotional condition. Indeed, images of disease start early, as Francisco confesses that he is "sick at heart" (1, 1, 9). The appearance of the Ghost of Hamlet's father reflects turmoil within the nation, as Horatio explains: "This bodes some strange eruption to our state" (1, 1, 80). What is particularly upsetting is that the apparition is armed, inspiring Horatio to explain the nation's recent military history: Old Hamlet defeated his great rival Fortinbras, but now his son, also named Fortinbras, is moving to avenge that defeat (1, 1, 91–119). The polarity between these two sons will be an ever-present burden for Hamlet.

When the Ghost reappears, Horatio poses three traditional explanations for its presence: "If there be any good thing to be done / That may do thee do ease and grace to me" (1, 1, 142–43); "If thou art privy to thy country's fate" (1, 1, 145); "Or if thou hast uphoarded in thy life / Extorted treasure in the womb of earth" (1, 1, 148–49). None of these hypotheses earns response.

Horatio also observes that at the sound of the cock crowing, the Ghost quickly leaves, and here is our first insinuation that it may be dangerous: "And then it started like a guilty thing / Upon a fearful summons" (1, 1, 163–64). Marcellus's observation about the Christmas season, when "no spirit dare stir abroad" (1, 1, 176), suggests that the Ghost is in opposition to Christian values, and this issue, too, becomes part of Hamlet's crisis.

As the action moves inside, Claudius mourns the recently deceased King Hamlet: "Though yet of Hamlet, our dear brother's death / The memory be green" (1, 2, 1–2). For the moment, he sounds reasonable: "With mirth in funeral and with dirge in marriage" (1, 2, 12). As he talks about his former sister-in-law, who has become his wife, he seems too smooth, so our suspicions might be aroused. Yet his calm dispatch of a letter to Fortinbras's uncle suggests a competent man in charge: "so much for him" (1, 2, 25). Lastly, after Polonius offers some pompous circumlocution (1, 2, 60–63), Claudius grants Laertes's request to return to Paris.

The first note of discord comes when Claudius addresses Hamlet as "my son" (1, 2, 66), a greeting that earns this multileveled aside from the prince: "A little more than kin and less than kind" (1, 2, 67). The intricate puns on *kin* (family) and *kind* (friendship) reveal Hamlet's brilliance as well as his bitterness over the royal marriage: "I am too much in the sun" (1, 2, 69), with *sun* being a traditional image of the kingship (as well as a pun on *son*).

Hamlet's anger moves to the fore when he answers his mother, who questions his extended state of mourning: "'Seems,' madam? Nay, it is. I know not 'seems'" (1, 2, 79). Later, he evinces a passion for "acting," with all the overtones that the word implies. He is also preoccupied with truth, and here we feel him probing Gertrude and Claudius for some revelation.

Soon we, too, will have questions about her: How much does she know about the death of her first husband? Does she suspect Claudius was involved? What was the relationship between Gertrude and Old Hamlet? What about between Claudius and Gertrude? We are also aware that currently we see all other characters through Hamlet's eyes. Subsequently, we will view those characters in private moments, but for now Shakespeare gives us the dramatic equivalent of a first-person narrative.

Claudius mildly chastises Hamlet for his "obstinate condolement" (1, 2, 97), but one other line from the speech stands out: "'Tis unmanly grief" (1, 2, 98). Claudius's implication is that Hamlet is weak or cowardly, an issue that torments Hamlet throughout the play. Claudius tries to bolster Hamlet's spirit with what the King claims is a magnanimous gesture: "You are the most immediate to our throne" (1, 2, 113). But in fact Hamlet's status has not changed at all. He remains as he was when his father was alive: next in the line of succession. Thus we wonder how much Hamlet's being denied the throne has contributed to his resentment.

Hamlet's first soliloquy expresses his inner state as best as he can articulate it, but the words may also be at least partially self-deceiving, an attempt to rationalize what pains him. Initially he is eager to commit suicide: "Or that the Everlasting had not fixed / His canon 'gainst self-slaughter!" (1, 2, 135–36). His attention quickly turns, however, to Denmark itself, where "Things rank and gross in nature / Possess it merely" (1, 2, 140–41). Underneath his anger lies frustration with his own powerlessness, and we sense that Hamlet regards himself as a failure, a condition for which he blames both the world and his own inadequacies.

One other fact gnaws at him, perhaps more than any other: his mother's sudden marriage to Claudius: "frailty, thy name is woman!" (1, 2, 150). As he attempts to articulate his fury, it overflows almost into incoherence:

> (O God, a beast that wants discourse of reason
> Would have mourned longer!),—married with my
>   uncle,
> My father's brother, but no more like my father
> Than I to Hercules. (1, 2, 154–58)

Conventional criticism suggests that in claiming that Claudius is entirely different from Hamlet's father, the prince is being truthful. But is he?

We know that old Hamlet was a respected commander, and from all that we have seen, so is Claudius. Hamlet also tells us that Gertrude loved his father, and she seems happy with Claudius. The two men were brothers; thus a degree of resemblance should be expected. Could Hamlet be offended that, after losing one militaristic, political man to his mother, he has now lost another? Hamlet, we soon learn, is a poet, a philosopher, and a playwright, utterly different from both of these men, who might reasonably regard him as a disappointment. Has Hamlet long felt his father's disapproval? And does that feeling complicate his tangled emotions?

The entrance of Horatio promotes a change within Hamlet, who at last has someone with whom he may share his animosity: "Thrift, thrift, Horatio. The funeral baked meats / Did coldly furnish forth the marriage tables" (1, 2, 187–88). When Horatio comments that old Hamlet was a "goodly king" (1, 2, 194), the prince reveals a little more of his attitude toward his father: "He was a man. Take him for all in all. / I shall not look upon his like again" (1, 2, 195–96). Is the last line ironic? Is Claudius more like his father than Hamlet cares to admit? Or even knows?

When Horatio reveals that the Ghost has appeared, Hamlet seeks, yet dreads, their meeting: "My father's spirit—in arms! All is not well. / I doubt some foul play" (1, 2, 277–78). *Doubt* here means *suspect*. We remember that Elizabethans of all classes believed in the power of ghosts to appear. Perhaps Hamlet hopes that such an encounter will confirm his own beliefs and also that that the ghost will give Hamlet's life purpose and therefore meaning.

Scene 3 is a reflection of the main action. After Laertes warns his sister Ophelia of the burdens Hamlet bears (1, 3, 17–27), Ophelia accepts this counsel but in turn warns Laertes not to be a hypocrite (1, 3, 50–55). Hypocrisy, however, is the way of this family, as Polonius demonstrates in his lengthy recitation of homilies. The last has particular resonance:

> This above all: to thine own self be true,
> And it must follow, as the night the day,
> Thou canst not then be false to any man. (1, 3, 84–86)

Polonius himself soon proves untrustworthy, but more to the point, how can any individual be true to one's "self" when that self is unclear? Such is part of Hamlet's dilemma. Polonius concludes with a warning about the dangers Hamlet poses (1, 3, 132–43), but despite her concession, Ophelia seems averse to ending her love so abruptly.

When we next see Hamlet, he bemoans the reputation of the kingdom: "They clepe us drunkards and with swinish phrase / Soil our addition" (1, 4, 21–22). Hamlet implies that Claudius bears guilt for this degeneration, but he has been king for only two months. Has Denmark long been this way, and is Claudius maintaining the tradition? Is Hamlet a puritan who finds any such behavior an affront?

He then comments on certain individuals forced to bear onerous obligations: "Carrying, I say, the stamp of one defect, / Being nature's livery or fortune's star" (1, 4, 34–35). The details also fit the Shakespearean tragic hero: thrust into circumstances he cannot control, possessed by qualities that under those circumstances prove fatal. The description, of course, will also apply to Hamlet himself.

When the ghost appears, Hamlet's immediate reaction is fear: "Angels and ministers of grace, defend us!" (1, 4, 43). Hamlet also has no idea how to interpret its presence: "Be thou a spirit of health or goblin damned" (1, 4, 44). Yet despite warnings from Horatio and Marcellus, Hamlet does not hesitate to follow the Ghost's beckoning: "I do not set my life at a pin's fee" (1, 4, 73). At the moment that life is meaningless, so Hamlet will welcome whichever answers the Ghost holds. Despite Horatio's protestation, Hamlet is determined: "My fate cries out" (1, 4, 91). The line is a plea for guidance that will lift him out of his torpor.

Alone with Hamlet, the Ghost soon hints at potential evil: "I am thy father's spirit, / Doomed for a certain term to walk the night" (1, 5, 14–15) and suffer unspeakable horrors. Then he adds, "If thou didst ever thy dear father love" (1, 5, 29). Hamlet's reply, "O God!" (1, 5, 30), suggests that perhaps the Ghost has touched a painful truth, but the apparition plunges ahead: "Revenge his foul and most unnatural murder" (1, 5, 31). Hamlet's one-word echo reveals shock, but his next response is curiously delicate:

> Haste me to know 't, that I, with wings as swift
> As meditation or thoughts of love
> May sweep to my revenge. (1, 5, 35–37)

As the Ghost implies (1, 5, 38–41), Hamlet hardly sounds like an instrument of revenge.

Perhaps both men believe that Hamlet has let his father down before, and here the Ghost sounds oddly like Claudius. Again, we remember that old Hamlet was a warrior, while his son is an artistic, contemplative soul. True, he is a skilled swordsman, but we observe him only at sport, not in combat. Thus that father and son lived at odds is quite possible, even likely.

The report that Claudius killed old Hamlet confirms the prince's worst fears: "O, my prophetic soul!" (1, 5, 48). In thrilling detail, the Ghost describes how he was poisoned, but what torments him most is that Gertrude now sleeps with Claudius: "Let not the royal bed of Denmark be / A couch for luxury and damnèd incest" (1, 5, 89–90). Yet the Ghost does not want her hurt: "Leave her to heaven" (1, 5, 93). Both father and son maintain the same attitude toward Gertrude: They overflow with anger but wish to spare her.

After the Ghost leaves, Hamlet tries to incite himself into action: "Yea, from the table of my memory / I'll wipe away all trivial, fond records" (1, 5, 105–6). Hamlet wants to erase his past relationship with his father and at last prove himself worthy of being his father's son. Yet when rejoined by his friends, Hamlet seems to rave, as Horatio indicates: "These are but wild and whirling words, my lord" (1, 5, 148). Meanwhile the Ghost's command that the others must swear to secrecy distracts Hamlet further.

Why that directive from the Ghost? Perhaps he has little faith that his son will fulfill the assigned task, and in fact Hamlet does seem overwhelmed: "There are more things in heaven and earth, Horatio, / Than are dreamt of in your philosophy" (1, 5, 187–88). His solution, then, as he mumbles almost incoherently, is "To put an antic disposition on" (1, 5, 192). What is his strategy? Why the need for delay?

Here is the crux of the play, which follows the long tradition of revenge drama. The genre began with the Roman dramatist Seneca and usually involves a single character who pursues an inexorable path of revenge that proves more destructive than the original act that inspired it. The reason for such revenge is almost always clear. Here, however, the task is confused beyond solution. Does the Ghost want Hamlet to commit revenge through murder? Perhaps, but Hamlet is simply not a killer.

Moreover, his feelings about his dead father are a mixture of love, fear, and possibly enmity. He loves his mother but hates how she lives with the uncle he despises. The court of Elsinore is in his hands, for he must purify not only the royal family but also the state of Denmark. Finally, as in all medieval and Renaissance revenge plays, the action involves the secular act of murder versus the Christian belief of letting divine providence carry out punishment.

Resolving all these conflicts is impossible: "The time is out of joint. O cursèd spite / That ever I was born to set it right!" (1, 5, 210–11). He has no idea what to do. But can we even try to answer for him? Is murder ever justifiable? As long as Hamlet resists, he has our sympathy. When, however, he capitulates that sympathy weakens, but never disappears entirely, for in Hamlet we see a man acting against his own nature.

In 2, 1, Polonius continues his hypocritical ways, dwelling on the debaucheries that he earlier decried and that might have been committed by his son: "Ay, or drinking, fencing, swearing, / Quarreling, drabbing—you may go so far" (2, 1, 28–29). Marcellus protests that reporting such behavior would damage Laertes, but Polonius ignores these niceties: "But breathe his faults so quaintly / That they may seem the taints of liberty" (2, 1, 34–36). He appears to be reliving his own youthful escapades.

When Polonius is joined by Ophelia, attention switches back to Hamlet, who, Ophelia warns, is dressed: "As if he had been loosèd out of hell / To speak of horrors" (2, 1, 93–94). In addition: "He falls to such perusal of my face / As he would draw it" (2, 1, 102–3). For what is Hamlet searching? Is he now acting mad? Or has he fallen into madness? Is he looking for a resemblance to his mother? Does he believe he is acting but has actually slipped into his role? The possibilities are myriad. In any case, Polonius plans to report his conclusion to the king: "This is the very ecstasy of love / Whose violent property fordoes itself" (2, 1, 114–15).

Claudius, meanwhile, has engaged Rosencrantz and Guildenstern, two of Hamlet's old schoolfellows, to observe the prince. The two are apparently indistinguishable, as they speak in matching syllables (2, 2, 27–34), and the King and Queen even address them by their wrong names. At this moment, therefore, they are primarily comic entities, but more sinister qualities soon surface.

Here is an opportunity to mention that although this pair was long regarded as quintessential nonentities, they have, thanks to British playwright Tom Stoppard's ingenious *Rosencrantz and Guildenstern Are Dead* (1967), become celebrated contemporary antiheroes. Indeed, *Hamlet* and Stoppard's version are now sometimes presented in repertory, with the same actors playing the same roles in both works. One of Stoppard's themes is that Rosencrantz and Guildenstern know nothing about either a murder or a marriage, and therefore they are more confused than everyone else as to what is happening. In a way, they become mini-Hamlets.

When Rosencrantz and Guildenstern leave, Polonius makes his report, leading the Queen to propose this explanation for Hamlet's behavior: "I doubt it is no other but the main— / His father's death and our o'erhasty marriage" (2, 2, 59–60). Do these lines reflect a spark of conscience? She is sensitive to these possibilities, but we still have no indication as to her feelings, knowledge, or previous actions. Meanwhile, when Voltemand brings a letter requesting permission for Fortinbras's troops to cross Danish territory, the King is too distracted by Hamlet to deal with the matter (2, 2, 86–91).

Polonius's reading of Hamlet's bizarre poem to Ophelia (2, 2, 117–30) confirms the court's apprehensions about the prince's mind. Such fears intensify when Polonius speaks with Hamlet, who is dressed peculiarly and spouting obscene remarks, especially about Ophelia:

> Conception is a
> blessing, but, as your daughter may conceive,
> friend, look to 't. (2, 2, 201–3)

When Hamlet inserts comments about how old men are not to be trusted (2, 2, 214–22), Polonius is befuddled but still analyzes: "Though this be madness, yet there is method in 't" (2, 2, 223–24).

We recognize (at least we think we do) that part of Hamlet's behavior here is a performance, but that he can flip back and forth casually between satirical remarks and what seems like aimless chatter suggests that he is still in control. Yet his capacity to alternate from wit to melancholy so quickly also points to a tenuous state of mind, one liable to deviate from rationality at any time.

Hamlet continues such banter with Rosencrantz and Guildenstern, tossing obscure remarks and references that leave his erstwhile friends baffled. At moments, however, his temper flashes: "Were you not sent for"? (2, 2, 295). He repeats that question several times, until suddenly he switches perspectives to one of solemnity: "I have of late, but wherefore I know not, lost all my mirth" (2, 2, 318–19), and he continues to explain that his mood has darkened.

Still, he remains capable of idealism: "What a piece of work is a man" (2, 2, 327). The rest of this statement is eloquent but bewildering. Even as Hamlet reveals his disillusion, he praises the world that leaves him dissatisfied. He thereby confirms that he wishes he were not so unhappy, that he is pretending to be so to excuse himself from his assignment, whatever he believes that to be.

The announcement that the players have arrived puts Hamlet in a happier frame of mind, but two comments remind us of his general condition. In one, he speaks of his "uncle-father and aunt-mother" (2, 2, 399). In the other, he notes, "I am but mad north-north-west" (2, 2, 402). He thus asserts that he can be sane when he chooses. That last phrase, by the way, was adapted by Alfred Hitchcock for one of his most celebrated films, coincidentally about a man caught in a maze of intrigue and whose identity is under attack.

When the players enter, Hamlet asks them to perform a portion about Pyrrhus, the son of Achilles who is called on to avenge his father's death. The parallel to Hamlet is obvious, but where Hamlet so far has failed, Pyrrhus succeeded. Seemingly inspired, Hamlet asks the players to perform *The Murder of Gonzago* with interpolations that he will provide (2, 2, 566–69). If Claudius responds as Hamlet expects, Hamlet will be reassured that the Ghost is honest. We must, however, pose a question: If Hamlet already believes the Ghost, why carry out this charade? The answer lies in the soliloquy that follows.

He feels humiliated that an actor in performance can summon the depth of feeling that Hamlet himself cannot: "But I am pigeon-livered and lack gall" (2, 2, 604). Thus he conceives a plan. What he cannot do in life, act on behalf of his father's spirit, he will enact on the stage of Elsinore and thereby find relief from his position as real-life avenger in his self-created role as theatrical avenger. He still has anxiety about the Ghost: "The spirit that I have seen / May be a devil" (2, 2, 627–28), but now he has a way to resolve those doubts: "I'll observe his looks; / I'll tent him to the quick" (2, 2, 625–26).

When Rosencrantz and Guildenstern report their failure to discern anything about Hamlet's behavior, a line from Ophelia's reading strikes the king: "How smart a lash that speech doth give my conscience" (3, 1, 57–58). Here begins one of the most fascinating twists of the play. For the first time, Claudius shows remorse. He is therefore not beyond sensibility, and the more we learn of him and the more we observe Hamlet's growing disassociation from humanity, the more we may develop sympathy for the King and lose it for the Prince. Meanwhile, as Hamlet arrives, Claudius and Polonius withdraw. Do they overhear the following scene?

The next soliloquy opens with the most famous line in world literature: "To be or not to be—that is the question" (3, 1, 64). Despite our overall uncertainty, we understand that Hamlet's strategies are in suspension, and he finds himself thinking to the point of inertia. He contemplates suicide but fears eternal consequence. Ironically, he uses the same word that Claudius did earlier: "Thus conscience does make cowards of us all" (3, 1, 91). Claudius used it to mean *guilt*, while Hamlet means his moral and psychological network that prevents action. Nevertheless, the two may have more in common than either thinks.

From this point on, Hamlet's mood alternates. When he mocks others, he is satiric. When he mocks himself, he is melancholy. But throughout this scene, we wonder how much he is acting, how much he is exposing his true feelings, and how much he is performing for the two men who may be observing. Indeed, we wonder how much self-mastery he has at all. We especially wonder about his feelings for Ophelia, but all we can say for sure is that his sexual fury is emerging.

He also seems to try to inspire himself to action:

> I am
> very proud, revengeful, ambitious, with more offenses
> at my beck than I have thoughts to put them
> in, imagination to give them shape, or time to act
> them in. (3, 1, 134–38)

He realizes that his attacks on Ophelia, his declarations of love that he simultaneously proclaims and withdraws, all amount to nothing, even though we feel his anger toward women in general: "God hath given you one face, and you / make yourselves another" (3, 1, 155–56). Yet no matter how brutally he treats her, he still cannot fulfill the Ghost's command.

When Hamlet departs, Ophelia muses on his behavior: "O, what a noble mind is here o'erthrown!" (3, 1, 164). The speech foreshadows her imminent breakdown. Claudius then advances with his own interpretation: "There's something in his soul / O'er which his melancholy sits on brood" (3, 1, 178–79). Claudius never romanticizes Hamlet's actions but rather quite practically seeks a solution. That comes from Polonius, who proposes sending Hamlet to England.

Hamlet's instructions to the players remain perhaps the best lesson for actors and directors ever formalized, but one portion has ramifications beyond the stage: "Suit the action to the word, the word to the action" (3, 2, 18–19). Hamlet, unfortunately, will not obey this dictum. Before the play begins, however, he bemoans his situation (3, 2, 76–79), then explains his plan to Horatio:

> If his occulted guilt
> Do not itself unkennel in one speech,
> It is a damnèd ghost that we have seen. (3, 2, 85–87)

He has never expressed skepticism before. Is the entire presentation to follow just one more tactic for delay?

Before the show begins, Hamlet greets each arrival with remarks aimed at fulfilling their explanations for his attitude. To Claudius, he talks about being "promise-crammed," implying frustrated ambition. To Polonius, he comments about Julius Caesar, with a pun on a "brute" killing. (One inside joke for Shakespeare's audience: The same actor who played Hamlet, Richard Burbage, probably played Brutus, and here he speaks to the actor who almost certainly played Caesar.) To Ophelia, Hamlet makes bawdy remarks about "country matters" (3, 2, 123), while to Gertrude, he talks about how long an interval has passed since his father died.

His antics continue during the performances, as he darts through the audience inserting remarks. Earlier, at the end of his second soliloquy, he asserted: "The play's the thing / Wherein I'll catch the conscience of the King" (2, 2, 633–34). But now, even though the king rushes out in dismay at seeing his crime enacted on stage, Hamlet so confounds other observers that they can only conclude that the king's discomposure was caused by Hamlet's behavior. Even Horatio can say no more than "I did very well note him" (3, 2, 316). Moreover, what has Hamlet learned? Events at the play merely confirmed what the Ghost had told him, so the result is further delay.

In the subsequent scene with Rosencrantz and Guildenstern, that pair assume a more active role, questioning with greater intensity, "The Queen your mother, in most great affliction of spirit, hath sent me to you" (3, 2, 339–40). For a few moments, Hamlet maintains a light tone, but as he did earlier with Ophelia, he bursts into anger that we should accept as legitimate: "Why, look you now, how unworthy a thing / you make of me!" (3, 2, 393–94). His "playing" has left him exhausted.

After more wordplay with Polonius that focuses on distorted perception, Hamlet seems to stir into action: "Now could I drink hot blood" (3, 2, 422–23). After he resolves to visit his mother, we realize that we have never seen the two of them alone together. Nonetheless, Hamlet is convinced that he can obey the ghost's order and discipline himself: "I will speak daggers to her, but use none" (3, 2, 429).

Another turning point occurs in 3, 3. First, Rosencrantz reminds Claudius of the scope of a king's influence:

> The cess of majesty
> Dies not alone, but like a gulf doth draw
> What's near it with it. (3, 3, 16–18)

Surely Rosencrantz intends to flatter Claudius by invoking the sacred position of a king, but the effect is the opposite, for Claudius knows he came by the throne through regicide, the murder of a legitimate king. Thus when left alone, he relives his monumental sin: "It hath the primal eldest curse upon 't, / a brother's murder" (3, 3, 41–42).

His is also aware that he should not expect forgiveness: "That cannot be, since I am still possessed / Of those effects for which I did the murder" (3, 3, 57–58). His escape from his suffering will come not on earth but in heaven (3, 3, 64–68). He seeks salvation but is helpless to do anything to achieve it. He wants to act but waits for something or someone to direct him. The parallel to Hamlet is unmistakable.

As Claudius kneels in prayer, Hamlet enters, and their role-switching becomes more painful for us. Initially, Hamlet realizes that here is his opportunity to fulfill the Ghost's directive, but killing Claudius under these circumstances will send him to heaven (3, 3, 77–93), an unacceptable resolution. Instead Hamlet resolves to wait: "When he is drunk asleep, or in his rage, / Or in th' incestuous pleasure of his bed" (3, 3, 94–95).

Throughout the play, we have felt the tension between Hamlet's role as mortal avenger and the Christian principle that ultimate judgment belongs to God. Hamlet now exceeds his earthly bounds and in doing so attempts to become a divine force, free to act without boundaries of morality and justice. In overstepping these limitations, however, he commits a terrible transgression of his own.

The encounter between Hamlet and Gertrude quickly turns violent. After he forces her to sit, the hidden Polonius, as ever plotting, makes sufficient noise that Hamlet impulsively stabs the arras. In his excitement, he accuses Gertrude: "A bloody deed—almost as bad, good mother, / As kill a king and marry with his brother" (3, 4, 34–35). Gertrude's response reflects shock at the accusation: "As kill a king?" (3, 4, 36), but leaves us no closer to understanding what she knows. Hamlet's attitude toward Polonius, however, tells a lot: "Thou wretched, rash, intruding fool, farewell. / I took thee for thy better" (3, 4, 38–39). He is viciously unrepentant.

Hamlet's tirade against his mother continues, with particular emphasis on her sexuality. Pointing to pictures of Claudius and old Hamlet, he confirms our supposition that what pains him most about his father's death is not the immediate passing, the loss of the throne, or thwarted love for Ophelia, but Gertrude's relationship with Claudius:

> You cannot call it love, for at your age
> The heyday in the blood is tame, it's humble
> And waits upon the judgment; and what judgment
> Would step from this to this? (3, 4, 78–81)

The thought of her desires repulses him.

Gertrude seems ready to confess: "O, Hamlet, speak no more! / Thou turn'st my eyes into my very soul" (3, 4, 99–100), but Hamlet does not stop attacking, so we can never be sure what she will reveal. Only when the Ghost appears does Hamlet relent, but the words he directs to an entity Gertrude cannot see baffle her: "This is the very coinage of your brain" (3, 4, 157). Still, Gertrude admits some misdeed, although we cannot confirm the precise reasons for her emotions: "O Hamlet, thou has cleft my heart in twain!" (3, 4, 177). Of all the questions that pervade *Hamlet*, the mystery of Gertrude's feelings may be the most tantalizing.

Hamlet's priority remains her physical desires, which he orders her to suppress (3, 4, 186–93), although how her doing so will help Hamlet is not clear. He then turns his attention to Polonius:

> I do repent; but heaven hath pleased it so
> To punish me with this and this with me,
> That I must be their scourge and minister. (3, 4, 194–96)

From the initial encounter with the Ghost, Hamlet has struggled to absolve himself from the task assigned. He has feigned madness, he has arranged for the play, and he has accused his mother. Now he claims to be at the mercy of other forces, an extension of heaven. Therefore in his mind he is absolved of moral consequences. In other words, he declares himself free.

This new attitude becomes manifest in his plan to deal with Rosencrantz and Guildenstern, whom he trusts, he says, as "adders fanged" (3, 4, 226). He knows they have been charged with taking him to England, along with letters that probably will lead to his death, so he resolves to undermine them. Meanwhile, he will remove Polonius's body: "I'll lug the guts into the neighbor room" (3, 4, 235), and jokes about Polonius's being "most grave" (3, 4, 237). His humor grows ever bleaker.

Act 4 is a bit chaotic, as the complexities Shakespeare has created seem to run wild. Nevertheless, the first scene propels the play forward as Gertrude tells Claudius what occurred in her chamber. Does her conscience continue to torment her? Even under this tension, though, we enjoy a comic moment with Rosencrantz and Guildenstern. Responding to the King's summons, they enter as if they have been waiting outside the room. After he directs them to locate Polonius's body, we imagine the two staring at each other wordlessly, shrugging, then departing in utter befuddlement.

That confusion continues in the next scene with Hamlet, as the Prince compares them to a sponge: "Ay, sir, that soaks up the King's countenance, his rewards, his authorities" (4, 2, 15–16). He wants them to understand that he does not trust them. In 4, 3, as the pair bring the Prince to Claudius, the repartee that follows is grimly funny, as Hamlet retorts that Polonius is at supper: "Not where he eats, but where he is eaten" (4, 3, 22). When the King completes the inquisition, he instructs Rosencrantz and Guildenstern to escort Hamlet to England, whereupon the two leave, on their way to becoming victims of a plot that was always beyond them.

The depths to which Hamlet has fallen are apparent in scene 4, when he meets the Norwegian captain and reflects in soliloquy on the military advances conducted by Fortinbras: "Witness this army of such mass and charge, / Led by a delicate and tender prince" (4, 4, 50–51). Fortinbras is a killer of the first order, but a frustrated Hamlet romanticizes the slaughter of war (4, 4, 55–68). He even invokes *honor*, a word that in Shakespeare often inspires foolish or immoral actions: "My thoughts be bloody or be nothing worth!" (4, 4, 69). Violence has become its own reward.

For the final scenes of act 4 Hamlet is absent, but his influence remains. On hearing about Ophelia's distress, for instance, Gertrude speaks of her own misery: "To my sick soul (as sin's true nature is), / Each toy seems prologue to some great amiss" (4, 5, 22–23). Although Hamlet's accusations are ingrained within her, we still do not know the precise crimes she believes she has committed.

Meanwhile, Ophelia enters, completely distracted while muttering lines and singing lyrics that suggest she has embraced the wanton sexuality that Hamlet assigned to her (3, 1, 131–32). The King believes he understands: "O, this is the poison of deep grief. It springs / All from her father's death" (4, 5, 80–81). Her breakdown illuminates Hamlet's battle, for under similar pressure he has maintained some equilibrium. Claudius notes further consequences: "Divided from herself and her fair judgment, / Without the which we are pictures or mere beasts" (4, 5, 92–93).

This description leads directly to the messenger's report that Laertes, infuriated at Polonius's death, has incited the rabble, who call him "lord" (4, 5, 112). Even when Laertes enters with forces, Claudius takes refuge behind the holy position of king: "There's such divinity doth hedge a king / That treason can but peep to what it would" (4, 5, 138–39). Laertes, however, shows no hesitation to rebel: "To hell, allegiance! Vows to the blackest devil! / Conscience and grace, to the profoundest pit!" (4, 5, 149–50).

In seeking revenge for his father, Laertes shows no inner conflict. Instead he threatens to unleash anarchy on the country. Only the presence of Ophelia, again painfully distracted, calms her brother, who also requires the soothing political touch of Claudius. The King denies responsibility for Polonius's death and invites Laertes to investigate, even at the risk of Claudius's losing his kingdom. Laertes accepts the terms but insists that Hamlet's death must follow. Everyone seems to seek some form of expiation.

In 4, 6, Horatio reads a letter from Hamlet about his adventure with pirates, an unwieldy plot device that nonetheless reflects Hamlet's efforts in a situation that demands the energy he has not been able to summon at court. Laertes again calls for Hamlet's death, but Claudius is reluctant to do anything that would hurt Gertrude (4, 7, 13–18) or offend the public, who regards Hamlet with affection.

Claudius's scheme gives further evidence of his ruthlessness. He overtly flatters Laertes, describing Hamlet's jealousy (which we assume is imaginary), then urges Laertes to quick action. Laertes suggests killing Hamlet in church, but Claudius's misgiving has a familiar ring: "No place indeed should murder sanctuarize" (4, 7, 145). We remember Hamlet's similar reaction to the prospect of murdering the praying Claudius. No matter how different the two men are, the act of murder draws them together spiritually.

Claudius then outlines his plan for a duel between Hamlet and Laertes. The poisoned wine and the envenomed tip of the sword are both tactics that could easily go astray or cast shadows on these two men, but each is desperate to rid himself of Hamlet, and thus they draw plans carelessly. Their distress grows greater with news from Gertrude that Ophelia has drowned. The details the Queen provides (4, 7, 190–208) make us question why no one rescued the girl, but even so we understand that here is another death for which Hamlet must accept blame. This one, however, is of someone whom he may have genuinely loved.

As act 5 begins, the tone changes once more. The two gravediggers (called "clowns") provide comic relief, but their banter has serious implications: "But if the water come to him and drown him, he drowns not himself" (5, 1, 18–19). Perhaps the gravedigger's offhand remarks hint that Hamlet is the victim of forces greater than himself and therefore not culpable for what has happened to him and to those around him. The gravedigger also reflects on the status of all men who eventually come before him (5, 1, 30–32), another theme that Hamlet soon echoes.

When he and Horatio enter, their tone is more informal than we have heard, especially as they muse about the gravedigger's casual attitude toward the remains:

> How the knave jowls it to the ground as if
> 'twere Cain's jawbone, that did the first murder!
> This might be the pate of a politician which this ass
> now o'erreaches, one that would circumvent God,
> might it not? (5, 1, 78–82)

The image obviously suggests Claudius, but someone else also comes to Hamlet's mind: "Or of a courtier, which could say 'Good morrow, sweet lord! How dost thou, sweet lord?'" (5, 1, 84–85). The subject sounds like Polonius or perhaps Rosencrantz and Guildenstern. Hamlet cannot stop ruminating over these men.

Another skull, which Hamlet imagines to be that of a lawyer, inspires further reflection on the transience of life: "Where be his quiddities now, his quillities, his cases, his tenures, and his tricks?" (5, 1, 101–2). Hamlet wants to believe that all human effort is pointless because under such circumstances all that he has been told to do is equally meaningless. Thus his failure may be excused.

The subsequent conversation with the gravedigger brings out a few intriguing points. One, the gravedigger has been at his job since "that very day that young Hamlet was born" (5, 1, 152–53), thirty years ago. Audiences often think of Hamlet as a teenager, but here he is identified as what in Shakespeare's day would have been practically middle-aged. Two, we hear the uncomfortable reminder that on the very day we're born, we start to die.

The disclosure that a particular skull is that of Yorick, the king's jester, leads Hamlet to cogitate further on how quickly life passes: "Alas, poor Yorick! I knew him, Horatio—" (5, 1, 190–91). It also reminds us that the most familiar picture of any actor who portrays Hamlet is one in which he broods over that skull. Such contemplation leads Hamlet to reflect on another prince, Alexander, who conquered the world but about whose remains Hamlet asks, " might they stop a beer barrel?" (5, 1, 219). One line later, Hamlet notes that even Julius Caesar's accomplishments have faded. Why, then, should Hamlet worry about the point of his own life?

At the sight of Ophelia's funeral procession, Hamlet is shocked, but that shock turns to outrage when Laertes jumps into the grave. The sight of two men fighting in the pit is grotesque, but what strikes us more is Hamlet's claim: "I loved Ophelia" (5, 1, 285). Whom is he trying to convince? By any measure he chooses, his existence has been a failure, and now he must acknowledge that he has cost yet another life. Perhaps that outcry is a last attempt to prove that a vestige of human feeling remains within him.

A similar expression of futility appears from Hamlet in the next scene: "There's a divinity that shapes our ends, / Rough-hew them how we will" (5, 2, 11–12). He concludes that providence is to blame for his failure. He even shrugs off responsibility for the deaths of Rosencrantz and Guildenstern because while in their company he had his royal signet: "Why, even in that was heaven ordinant" (5, 2, 54). Thus he rewrote the letter that ordered his death and caused the bearers to be executed. Horatio questions such morality, but Hamlet is immune to incertitude:

> They are not near my conscience. Their defeat
> Does by their own insinuation grow.
> 'Tis dangerous when the baser nature comes
> Between the pass and fell incensèd points
> Of mighty opposites. (5, 2, 65–69)

In Hamlet's eyes, he and Claudius are now "mighty opposites."

The obsequious Osric, whom Hamlet mocks for apparent effeminacy, brings a bit more comic relief but also a challenge from the King to duel Laertes. While Osric claims that Claudius supports Hamlet (5, 2, 178–85), Horatio worries for Hamlet's safety. The Prince, meanwhile, is resigned to the worst: "There is a special providence in the fall of a sparrow" (5, 2, 233–34). Life has exhausted him, and he welcomes death as deliverance. His tone is noble, but underlying it is acceptance of the absurdity of existence.

When the audience gathers, Hamlet's apology to Laertes focuses on the Prince's supposed madness (5, 2, 245–58), but we understand a different version of Hamlet's life. After other forces took over, he never was able to take charge of himself, and the result was catastrophe on many levels. His personal qualities and the demands of his position clashed and in the process defeated him.

In the carnage of the final scene, several moments stand out. One, at the King's behest, Osric gives each man a sword, and we wonder whether Osric, also the referee of the bout, is an accessory to the King's intrigue. Two, Gertrude's giddy participation by drinking reflects her acceptance of what has happened in Elsinore. Just as she married Claudius and contributed to the general decay of her court, so now, after Claudius poisons the wine, she "carouses" (5, 2, 315) to Hamlet's fortune. Three, as Laertes prepares to strike with the envenomed sword, he hesitates: "And yet it is almost against my conscience" (5, 2, 324). We remember when the word was used by both Claudius (3, 1, 58) and Hamlet (3, 1, 91).

When the dying Laertes accuses Claudius of poisoning the sword that cuts Hamlet, as well as the drink that kills Gertrude, Hamlet at last summons the anger to stab the King, but so respected is the throne that onlookers shout: "Treason, treason!" (5, 2, 354). Nevertheless, Hamlet violently forces Claudius to drink the poison. Mere murder is no longer enough, as all the anger in him emerges (5, 2, 376–84). Yet even as Hamlet begins to expire, he urges Horatio to resist the convenient escape of suicide. Hamlet wants his story told, as if through narrative art it will acquire meaning.

In his last lines, Hamlet, very briefly as King, restores order by anointing the approaching Fortinbras to the throne. Another militaristic ruler takes power. When Fortinbras does arrive, Horatio explains what has taken place but ignores Hamlet's role in the deaths of Rosencrantz and Guildenstern. In an unintentionally ironic gesture, Fortinbras orders soldiers to "Bear Hamlet like a soldier" (5, 2, 442), an inappropriate end for such a man. Even the play's last line, "Go, bid the soldiers shoot" (5, 2, 449), confirms that the values of this society have not changed.

The perplexities posed by Hamlet and *Hamlet* are almost unfathomable. We have a hero whose political, social, ethical, religious, artistic, familial, and sexual quandaries leave him completely disenfranchised from the human community. He never does decide "Who's there?" (1, 1, 1). Yet his struggle to answer that question and thereby join that community makes him the embodiment of the alienation and consequent search for identity that all of us at some time undergo. For Hamlet, though, the quest is one he bears at every moment of his life. Therefore, like existence itself, he is forever a puzzle.

Chapter Four

Othello

One famous, if apocryphal, story about *Othello* concerns a nineteenth-century actor-director who cast himself in the title role, then hired a costar of equal stature to enact Iago. The morning after the opening, all reviews praised Iago and ignored Othello. For his next production of the play, the same actor-director hired a relative unknown for Iago, but this man, too, garnered the good notices. Finally, for his next go-round, the actor-director took on Iago himself and received raves. Such is the power of that character.

Iago is perhaps the outstanding example of the Machiavel, a compelling class of villain. In any literary or dramatic work, "bad guys" are often the most intriguing personages because their desire to obtain money, power, or some other goal provides the intellectual and emotional energy that propels the plot. Moreover, they almost always conceive the plan to fulfill that desire and to which heroes and heroines respond.

The antecedent of the Machiavel is the vice figure from medieval morality plays, and the name is taken from Niccolò Machiavelli (1469–1527), the Italian statesman whose book *Il Principe* (*The Prince*, 1513) contributed profoundly to the Renaissance view of political realism. Even today, Machiavelli's advice on the administration of effective government remains synonymous with perfidious manipulation.

What gives Machiavels a unique flavor is that they relish their unscrupulousness. In addition, their wit, in combination with freedom from moral restraint, creates an allure that is aimed toward despicable ends but is also theatrically gripping. We enjoy seeing Machiavels operate. We plot with them and laugh with them. And when they are not onstage, we miss them. (At this point in the discussion, feel free to ask the class for Machiavels from contemporary works. Any villain from a James Bond film will do, and no doubt students will suggest others.)

Which brings us to Iago. He is perhaps the supreme Machiavel but with one qualifier. In Shakespeare's source for the play (Cinthio's short story "Tale of the Moor," 1565), Iago is jealous of Othello and seeks Disdemona [*sic*] for his own. In *Othello*, Iago's motivation is less explicit and may be based on race, sexual desire, professional promotion, or some combination thereof. The great English poet Samuel Coleridge (1772–1834) attributed Iago's behavior to "motiveless malignity," but such analysis is ultimately unsatisfactory, especially for characters that must be performed. Just as people act as they do for a reason, so do well-conceived characters.

That uncertainty is apparent in 1, 1, when Iago listens to Roderigo complain about Desdemona's marriage to Othello. Accused of treachery for not helping Roderigo, Iago protests that he hates the Moor, who left Iago at the rank of ensign and promoted Michael Cassio: "A fellow almost damned in a fair wife" (1, 1, 22). (The precise meaning of this description is unknown, but it is surely not flattering.)

Indeed, Iago resents any kind of subservience, especially to Othello: "I follow him to serve my turn upon him" (1, 1, 45). And later: "Were I the Moor I would not be Iago. / In following him, I follow but myself" (1, 1, 63–64). While Iago thereby sets himself as an enemy to the social order, he offers one possible reason for his later actions: failure to achieve professional advancement.

Yet that rationale proves unconvincing. First, Iago never again dwells on promotion. Indeed, he never concerns himself with business of the world. Second, his immediate preoccupation is upsetting the marriage between Desdemona and Othello, but even here, his motivation is not clear. Rather, he speaks of his "peculiar end" (1, 1, 66), as if he himself cannot specify what he hopes to gain.

To begin his intrigue, he directs Roderigo to stir up trouble by calling Brabantio, Desdemona's father: "Rouse him. Make after him, poison his delight" (1, 1, 75). Here is the first of numerous references to poison that highlights Iago's dialogue. When Brabantio appears, Iago, unseen in darkness, shouts a warning that reveals another aspect of his character: "Even now, now, very now, an old black ram / Is tupping your white ewe" (1, 1, 97–98). The repetition of *now* has an unnerving energy, as if Iago were trying to make Brabantio feel the sexual experience vicariously.

The cry should also be understood as a reflection of Iago's mind. He is outraged by the relationship between the white Desdemona and the black Othello and continually portrays it in brutal terminology. Interestingly, all his comments about sexuality are spiced with pornographic rudeness, and thus we must consider whether his inner wound, the cause of his anger, is sexual in nature.

Brabantio dismisses Roderigo as unworthy (1, 1, 106–12) but still cannot believe that his daughter has committed such an act: "This is Venice. My house is not a grange" (1, 1, 119), foreshadowing the conflict between civilization and barbarism that pervades the play. But Iago maintains his barrage:

> I am one, sir, that comes to tell you your daughter
> and the Moor are now making the beast with
> two backs. (1, 1, 129–31)

Brabantio soon takes to the streets for help: "Light, I say, light!" (1, 1, 160). Images of light and dark recur frequently, mirroring both the contrast between the white skin of Desdemona and the black skin of Othello, as well as the battle between the purity of the couple and the evil of Iago.

Once Brabantio has responded, Iago scurries away, with an excuse to Roderigo about appearing loyal to Othello, who is heading off to war (1, 1, 161–77). The truth is that Iago does not want to be discovered anywhere near these environs. Immediately after he leaves, Brabantio returns, vowing to find Othello but also confirming how effective Iago's tactics have been.

In 1, 2, the tone of the play changes as we meet Othello, who is called a Moor, a term used to describe a generic African. In response to Iago's warning about Brabantio, Othello appears self-assured: "My services which I have done the signiory / Shall out-tongue his complaints" (1, 2, 21–22). The rest of the speech suggests that he has never known failure. He has triumphed in war, and he is of noble stock. Therefore, he reasons, the world must respect him.

Yet the speech also reveals a curious naïveté, a willingness to trust society's sense of justice. He also is accustomed to working with military matters and solely among men, where he lives by a soldier's code of honor. Finally, he is inexperienced in any cosmopolitan setting, particularly a white setting and particularly among women, and his lack of sophistication will prove endemic to his downfall.

Cassio then rushes in to explain that Othello has been summoned to resolve a military crisis (1, 2, 46–55). When Othello retreats to his house, Iago explains about their commander's wife: "Faith, he tonight hath boarded a land carrack. / If it prove lawful prize, he's made forever" (1, 2, 60–61). Cassio fails to understand this oblique remark, so Iago mockingly simplifies: "He's married" (1, 2, 63). The innocence Cassio shows here will contribute to his undoing.

The scene shifts to the duke's chambers, in which we hear for the first time of the threat posed by the Turks in Cyprus, a colony of Venice. The intimation is that savages are infiltrating civilization, an action that parallels the intrusion of Iago into the relationship between Othello and Desdemona. Brabantio then rushes in to accuse Othello of having stolen Desdemona: "By spells and medicines bought of mountebanks" (1, 3, 74). The Moor humbly protests his innocence (1, 3, 91–111), and recounts tales from his life and Desdemona's reaction to a similar narrative:

> My story being done,
> She gave me for my pains a world of sighs.
> She swore, in faith, 'twas strange, 'twas passing
>   strange,
> 'Twas pitiful, 'twas wondrous pitiful. (1, 3, 182–86)

Pity in the Elizabethan context also suggests *love*.

Here is the crux of their relationship. Desdemona has fallen in love not with a man but with her image of a man. Nor does he really know her, as he admits: "She loved me for the dangers I had passed, / And I loved her that she did pity them" (1, 3, 193–94). The two have married as if they had fallen love with each other's portrait. Still, the intensity of their love impresses the Duke: "I think this tale would win my daughter, too" (1, 3, 197).

When Desdemona enters, her resolution is obvious: "My noble father / I do perceive here a divided duty" (1, 3, 208–9). She speaks evenly, without fear, for she knows exactly who she is. The force of her personality overwhelms Brabantio, who reluctantly withdraws his complaint (1, 3, 219–28). Othello is appointed to lead the conflict against the Turks, but his request to have Desdemona sheltered in his absence meets with a surprising objection from the woman herself:

> I saw Othello's visage in his mind,
> And to his honors and his valiant parts
> Did I my soul and fortunes consecrate. (1, 3, 287–89)

Here is another intimation that the two have fallen in love with each other's idealized vision.

Othello agrees to take her with him but senses uneasiness in his listeners: "I therefore beg it not / To please the palate of my appetite . . . But to be free and bounteous to her mind" (1, 3, 296–97, 300). We cannot be certain if he seeks to emphasize the spiritual side of their marriage or if he downplays the physical aspects to avoid causing offense. In any case, we may assume he is self-conscious about the racial difference between himself and Desdemona.

This section illuminates two aspects of Othello's personality. First, he may not be totally convinced of her devotion. At this moment, any doubt is miniscule, even subconscious, but we wonder if it exists from the start. Second, Othello is a black man in white Venice and therefore an alien. Despite his pride, he remains vulnerable to hints of fallibility, and when he becomes suspicious of Desdemona, he has no one in whom he may confide. Thus his apprehension turns inward, where it is intensified by his disconnect from the white environment.

In another moment that will have ironic repercussions, Othello requests that Iago escort Desdemona: "A man he is of honesty and trust" (1, 3, 323). Other characters also refer to Iago as honest, which has connotations of *simple*. Brabantio, however, issues a warning: "Look to her, Moor, if thou hast eyes to see. / She has deceived her father, and may thee" (1, 3, 333–34). Iago will recall this advice at a particularly opportune moment. In addition, imagery of sight recurs throughout, as differences between what Othello imagines and what he actually sees become pronounced. At this moment, though, his trust appears absolute: "My life upon her faith!" (1, 3, 335).

When Roderigo and Iago are alone, the former bemoans his predicament in love: "I will incontinently drown myself" (1, 3, 347), but Iago scoffs, "It is merely a lust of the blood and a permission of the will. Come, be a man!" (1, 3, 377–78). He disdains emotion and reduces all human behavior to the law of the jungle. He also sneers at affection, especially between a man and a woman: "When she is sated with his body, she will find the error of her choice" (1, 3, 393–94).

Why does Iago scorn women and sexuality? Several causes are apparent. One, as we shall see, he is trapped in a loveless marriage. Two, his estimate of his own value is not matched by his stature in the world, and because women do not find him attractive, he disdains them. Three, Iago must serve Othello, a black man in an apparently happy marriage and whose very existence emphasizes Iago's failures.

Driven by these impulses, he conducts a campaign against everything he wants to be but cannot be, everything that reminds him of his deficiencies and thereby exacerbates his humiliation. Because he cannot find happiness within himself, he works to mar the happiness of others. He delights in disorder, in playing the sycophant, and in subverting all institutions, social and moral.

How much of all this does Iago understand? His soliloquies suggest that he realizes very little. For instance, after Roderigo leaves, Iago rationalizes his hatred of Othello:

> I hate the Moor,
> And it is thought abroad that 'twixt my sheets
> 'Has done my office. I know not if 't be true,
> But I, for mere suspicion in that kind,
> Will do as if for surety. (1, 3, 429–33)

The conjecture that Othello has slept with Emilia is ludicrous, but Iago doesn't care. All he wants is to destroy, to show that because of Othello's and Desdemona's innate goodness, they are weaker than he. In his last two lines here, he puts his life in perspective: "I have 't. It is engendered. Hell and night / Must bring this monstrous birth to the world's light" (1, 3, 446–47). The word *monstrous* recurs often, an appropriate adjective for one who identifies with the devil.

In 2, 1, we go to Cyprus, a primitive colony of Venice, where Desdemona and Othello are more vulnerable to subversive forces. First, though, Cassio speaks about Othello and Desdemona:

> He hath achieved a maid
> That paragons description and wild fame,
> One that excels the quirks of blazoning pens,
> And in th' essential vesture of creation
> Doth tire the ingener. (2, 1, 67–71)

The flattery is excessive and suggests that Cassio's formality masks less noble instincts. Such deception, in tandem with his pride in rank, will recur.

The entrance of Desdemona, Emilia, and Iago provokes playful exchanges that we recognize as reflecting Iago's inner self. For instance, as Cassio kisses Emilia: "Sir, would she give you so much of her lips / As of her tongue she oft bestows on me" (2, 1, 112–13). Always he maintains a polite veneer, for a crucial ingredient in his success is the charm that helps him win the confidence of others. At the same time, he keeps plotting, as when Cassio takes Desdemona's hand: "With as little a web as this will I ensnare as great a fly as Cassio" (2, 1, 183–84).

When Othello enters, the informal environment of Cyprus seems to have allowed his manner to relax: "O, my fair warrior!" (2, 1, 197). Such a greeting to his wife is strange, but what he says next is even stranger: "If it were now to die, / 'Twere now to be most happy" (2, 1, 205–6). What seems like a statement of devotion is actually one of foreboding, for these two exist on such an exalted plane that they cannot withstand the buffets of reality.

Iago seems to recognize as much: "But I'll set down the pegs that make this music, / As honest as I am" (2, 1, 219–20). Throughout Shakespeare, images of music reflect social and political order, and various institutions are either "in tune" or suffer "dissonance." Here the disharmony Iago unleashes reflects the chaos that results, while the discord that Othello repels on the military front undermines his personal life.

Left alone again with Roderigo, who continues to pine for Desdemona, Iago dwells once more on what he imagines will be her inevitable rejection of Othello: "Her eye must be fed. And what delight shall she have to look on the devil" (2, 1, 246–47). Once more he slanders both husband and wife, and with the identical goal: to rationalize his failure with women, who, he claims, seek only physical pleasure. Hence he is right to spurn them.

After persuading Roderigo to start a fight with Cassio, supposedly a rival for Desdemona (2, 1, 288–92), Iago again confesses his convoluted feelings:

> Now, I do love her too,
> Not out of absolute lust (though peradventure
> I stand accountant for as great a sin)
> But party led to diet my revenge
> For that I do suspect the lusty Moor
> Hath leaped into my seat. (2, 1, 313–18)

Some critics suggest that this speech is evidence that Iago wants Desdemona for himself, but even as he asserts that possibility, he denies it because the only reason for that desire is lust, which he acknowledges, then disparages. He has affection for no one. If he truly wanted to possess Desdemona (or so he tells himself), the only reason would be to ruin her. Yet his dwelling on these feelings suggests that inside of him lurks desire of some kind.

Scene 2 establishes the spirit of revelry in Cyprus, but Othello tells Cassio to quash it: "Let's teach ourselves that honorable stop / Not to outsport discretion" (2, 3, 2–3). Unfortunately, the entrance of Iago assures that sobriety will not last. Dramatic tradition holds that a character who, like Cassio, warns everyone about his susceptibility to alcohol will soon drink, then suffer the consequences. Here Iago makes salacious remarks about Desdemona, creating a phony masculine bonhomie (2, 3, 15–30), and his next step is getting three Cypriot guards drunk to contribute to the state of dissipation.

Just as Cassio predicted, when rowdy songs and ditties are unleashed, he becomes intoxicated. He then staggers away, leaving Iago to explain to Montano that Cassio's condition is chronic: "'Tis evermore the prologue to his sleep" (2, 3, 134). Montano reflects that Othello must not be aware of Cassio's weakness:

> Perhaps he sees it not, or his good nature
> Prizes the virtue that appears in Cassio
> And looks not on his evils. (2, 3, 139–41)

In one more irony in a play filled with them, this description applies perfectly to Iago.

Word of the expected fight between Cassio and Roderigo at last reaches Othello, who is compelled to leave his home and quell the disorder: "Are we turned Turks, and to ourselves do that / Which heaven hath forbid the Ottomites?" (2, 3, 182–83). Native customs that the Venetians believe they have eradicated will infiltrate their society, while we discover that such instincts are latent in Othello himself.

With seeming reluctance, Iago explains that Cassio and Roderigo were as close as "bride and groom" (2, 3, 192), a malicious swipe at Othello's being forced to abandon his marriage bed. After confirmation by Montano, Othello reveals a hitherto unseen aspect of himself: "My blood begins my safer guides to rule" (2, 3, 219). Before long, this description proves ironically tragic, when his fury rises beyond control.

Iago continues to feign hesitation to accuse anyone; nonetheless, he soon blames the squabble on Cassio (2, 3, 235–61). Othello accepts this version and thereby foreshadows another betrayal: "Cassio, I love thee, / But nevermore be officer of mine" (2, 3, 264–65). How convenient for Iago that Desdemona enters at just this moment to witness Cassio's humiliation, for in a few moments she becomes part of Iago's larger scheme.

Left alone with Iago, Cassio berates himself: "O, I have lost my reputation!" (2, 3, 281–82), but Iago dismisses such sniveling: "You have lost no reputation at all, unless you repute yourself such a loser" (2, 3, 289–90). He even offers a plan based on appealing to Desdemona: "Our general's wife is now the general" (2, 3, 333–34). He is joking, but the line reflects his contempt for a man who shares his life with a woman. After pondering how to make Cassio's behavior with Desdemona suspicious enough to anger Othello, Iago summarizes his strategy:

> So I will turn her virtue into pitch,
> And out of her own goodness make the net
> That shall enmesh them all. (2, 3, 380–82)

Nothing pleases him so much as undermining an individual's most admirable qualities.

A "clown" is offered in 3, 1, for comic respite, but the character is superfluous in a play where Iago continually provides laughter, even if it is bitter, as when Cassio says of Iago, "I never knew / A Florentine more kind and honest" (3, 1, 43–45). Emilia then counsels Cassio that Desdemona "speaks for you stoutly" (3, 1, 49) and leads to one of Shakespeare's greatest scenes. It is virtually devoid of physical action, but the tension is overwhelming, so if opportunity permits, here is one episode to play for the class.

Immediately after Desdemona promises Cassio that she will speak on his behalf to her husband, Othello and Iago enter to see Cassio exit. Iago seizes the opportunity: "Ha, I like not that" (3, 3, 37). From here on, his every line is aimed at provoking Othello to jealousy, which leads to anger, which leads to madness. Throughout the scene, we return to a familiar question: Is this madness planted by Iago, or does the seed exist in Othello from the start, and does Iago merely cultivate it?

The next line that works on Othello comes seconds later:

> Cassio, my lord? No, sure, I cannot think it
> That he would steal away so guiltylike,
> Seeing your coming. (3, 3, 41–43)

This short speech contains several elegant touches, including *steal away* and *guiltylike*, as well as the insinuation that Cassio departed only because he saw Othello. Desdemona compounds the awkwardness by referring to Cassio as a "suitor" (3, 3, 46), as if unaware of the double meaning. Desdemona also pushes Othello, asking repeatedly when he will deal with Cassio. Othello attempts to calm her, but she is relentless: "Why, this is not a boon!" (3, 3, 85).

Although Othello reaffirms his willingness to discuss the matter later: "I will deny thee nothing!" (3, 3, 93), the repetition of this line makes him sound testy, as if he is embarrassed to have his authority questioned in front of Iago. When she leaves, though, he seems to regain control: "But I do love thee! And when I love thee not, / Chaos is come again" (3, 3, 101–2). He is ashamed to be curt with her, but the threat of chaos proves tragically accurate.

The rest of the scene creates an astonishing mixture of emotions in the audience. On the one hand, we are infuriated by Othello's vulnerability and the rage to which he succumbs. On the other, we reluctantly admire Iago's skill, insight, and wit. Thus the following lines from Othello leave us desperate to stop the action:

> By heaven, thou echo'st me
> As if there were some monster in thy thought
> Too hideous to be shown. (3, 3, 121–23)

Ironic overtones follow relentlessly, as Othello almost forces Iago to reveal his supposed suspicions: "By heaven, I'll know thy thoughts" (3, 3, 191).

Earlier, when Cassio bemoaned the loss of his reputation (2, 3, 281–82), Iago dismissed such concerns. Here he takes the opposite approach:

> But he that filches from me my good name
> Robs me of that which not enriches him
> And makes me poor indeed. (3, 3, 188–90)

Iago also cautions Othello against jealousy, the "green-eyed monster" (3, 3, 196). In the very next line, though, Iago inserts *cuckold* (3, 3, 197), which seems to drive Othello over the edge, even if he recovers momentarily: "No, Iago, / I'll see before I doubt" (3, 3, 220–21).

At this juncture, Iago invokes one of his most diabolic tactics by recalling Brabantio's warning: "She did deceive her father, marrying you" (3, 3, 238). Then, as if attempting to hypnotize Othello, Iago implies several times that Othello seems unnerved, but the Moor holds onto his confidence: "I do not think but Desdemona's honest" (3, 3, 265), a weak affirmation that Iago undercuts: "Long live she so! And long live you to think so!" (3, 3, 266). *Think* implies that what Othello wants to believe is false.

Despite such wavering, Othello still maintains faith in Desdemona until this moment: "And yet, how nature erring from itself" (3, 3, 267). *Yet* may be regarded as the climactic word of the play, for by admitting even the possibility that Desdemona has been unfaithful, Othello dooms himself, as Iago recognizes at once: "Ay, there's the point" (3, 3, 268). From here on, Iago emphasizes all the differences between Othello and Desdemona, spurring the Moor's insecurities.

After Iago's brief exit, Othello drives himself to distraction:

> O curse of marriage,
> That we can call these delicate creatures ours
> And not their appetites! (3, 3, 309–11)

These lines sound as if they came directly from Iago. Thus again we wonder if the "monster" inside his ensign also smolders within Othello. After Desdemona enters, Othello struggles to resist thoughts of her infidelity, so to alleviate what she imagines is some strange illness, she takes out her handkerchief and places it on his head.

As Othello shoves the handkerchief aside and the two of them leave, Emilia recognizes it as a love token from Othello that Iago has sought. We are not sure why he wants it, and neither is she, but we are even more puzzled that a few moments later she allows him to grab it. Indeed, for the rest of the play we have trouble understanding Emelia. Although she is worldly, especially about men, she allows herself to be manipulated by Iago. True, everyone else is as well, but she should know him best.

When Othello returns, raving more than ever and threatening to throttle Iago if he does not provide proof, Iago adds details: "It is impossible you should see this, / Were they as prime as goats, as hot as monkeys" (3, 3, 459–60). He then fashions an intimate image of himself lying with Cassio, who in his sleep supposedly muttered lasciviously about Desdemona, embraced Iago, and cursed Othello. The details are graphic: "And then, sir, would he gripe and wring my hand, / Cry 'O sweet creature!' then kiss me hard" (3, 3, 477–78). Is this fantasy a wish fulfillment?

The final detail is Cassio's wiping his beard with the handkerchief (3, 3, 498), a picture that sends Othello over the edge: "Arise, black vengeance, from the hollow hell!" (3, 3, 507). Iago then kneels, and Othello joins him in what looks like a mock marriage, capped by Iago's expression of devotion: "I am your own forever" (3, 3, 546). This action, in concert with the specificity of the dream, suggests another motivation for Iago's behavior: desire for Othello. Indeed, much of the play can be performed with Iago literally embracing him. Still, Emilia furnishes no evidence of Iago's having sexual leanings for Othello, nor does he in any of his soliloquies.

In scene 4, although Desdemona continues to search for the handkerchief, she does not worry that the loss will make Othello jealous (3, 4, 25–29). Emilia, however, reveals nothing, and again we speculate about her loyalty. When Othello enters, distracted and muttering to himself, his vocabulary is dominated by words laden with sexual overtones: "Hot, hot, and moist" (3, 4, 45). When he demands the handkerchief, he adds that "There's magic in the web of it?" Is he lying? Or was he lying before when he denied any magical properties (1, 3, 195)?

As Othello's demands for the handkerchief grow sharper, Desdemona's mentioning of Cassio unintentionally exacerbates her husband's anger, as manifest in the repetition of "The handkerchief!" (3, 4, 59) with greater violence, until Desdemona is bewildered by his ferocity. (Here is a moment to mention that actors sometimes speak of Othello as Shakespeare's most physically and vocally demanding part because from act 3 until the end, the character's emotions remain at the highest intensity.)

Emilia explains Othello's behavior:

> 'Tis not a year or two shows us a man.
> They are all but stomachs, and we all but food;
> They eat us hungerly, and when they are full
> They belch us. (3, 4, 120–23)

This analysis again leads us to wonder about Emilia. Is she jealous of Desdemona? Possibly she is angry at Othello. In any case, she could quickly resolve the confusion, but she chooses not to. Furthermore, her disdainful attitude toward sex is no doubt based on her marriage to Iago, whose own feelings have been warped by his relationship with her.

When Cassio, spurred by Iago, enters to solicit Desdemona's help once more, she demurs: "My advocation is not now in tune" (3, 4, 142). The line recalls Iago's earlier music imagery (2, 1, 219–20). Desdemona's remarks, meanwhile, allow Iago to divert attention from himself: "Is my lord angry?" (3, 4, 151), a pose of innocence bound to draw laughter from the audience. Desdemona is inclined to forgive her husband, but Emilia is not so generous:

> But jealous souls will not be answered so.
> They are not ever jealous for the cause,
> But jealous for they're jealous. It is a monster
> Begot upon itself, born on itself. (3, 4, 180–83)

We know that the "monster" exists inside Iago. Does it live in Othello as well?

Left alone, Cassio is joined by Bianca, who claims that he has not visited her for a week. Cassio's upright manner clashes with Bianca's earthy appeal, which he tries to assuage by presenting her with the handkerchief he found in his chamber. Then he hurries off, offering the explanation that Othello would not want to see him with a woman, although Cassio does not mention that Bianca might not meet with Othello's approval. Such deception and general weakness do not help Cassio's standing.

In 4, 1, Iago's words still torment Othello, who rages incoherently:

> Pish! Noses, ears, and
> lips—is 't possible? Confess—handkerchief—O,
> devil! (4, 1, 52–54)

He then falls into what we may assume is an epileptic fit, which provokes further sneering from Iago. Once Cassio has been dismissed, Othello awakens to more torment from Iago:

> Good, sir, be a man!
> Think every bearded fellow that's but yoked
> May draw with you. (4, 1, 81–83)

As usual, Iago's insinuation is a way not only to torture Othello but also to mock all married men.

At Iago's suggestion, Othello hides to overhear the subsequent conversation between Iago and Cassio, evidence of how low Othello has sunk. Cassio's eagerness to share with Iago lewd remarks about Bianca, as well as Cassio's weak attempt to placate her, shows that his puritanical demeanor is another deception. As Othello assumes that their subject is Desdemona, his temper explodes again: "Ay, let her rot and perish and be damned / tonight, for she shall not live" (4, 1, 202–3). Then he wails, "But yet the pity of it, / Iago! O, Iago, the pity of it, Iago!" (4, 1, 216–17), and we recall *pity* from Othello's early narrative (1, 3, 186).

After Othello again shouts about being made a cuckold, Iago toys further with him: "O 'tis foul in her!" which is followed by Othello's "With mine officer!" to which Iago mocks even more: "That's fouler" (4, 1, 222–24). We may find ourselves laughing against our will. But when Othello calls for poison, Iago's strategy is downright vicious: "Do it not with poison. Strangle her in her bed, even the bed she hath contaminated" (4, 1, 228–29). Why should Iago be so concerned? Because poison is, figuratively if not literally, his weapon. Strangling her, on the other hand, would amount to vicarious rape, as close as Iago can come to sexual gratification.

When Desdemona enters with her cousin Lodovico, she innocently asks about Cassio, setting off another outburst from Othello that climaxes in the most brutal moment of the play thus far, as he strikes her while shouting: "Devil!" (4, 1, 270). Now his accusations are public, while his fragmented explanation to one listener after another reflects his breakdown (4, 1, 286–98). The final "Goats and monkeys!" (1, 4, 297–98) confirms that Iago's metaphoric poison has done its job. The ensign's casual remarks, delivered, no doubt, with an appropriately sad expression, confirm that the upset in Othello's life has turned into chaos.

Othello's confrontation with Emilia is the first time these two are alone onstage, but little more is revealed, as Othello derogates her as a "subtle whore" (4, 2, 23). Othello continues to berate Desdemona, but what can she do? She cannot admit to a lie, but when she returns and denies wrongdoing, he asserts that she is lying: "Therefore be double damned / Swear thou art honest" (4, 2, 44–46). His harangue builds to one unbearable line: "I took you for that cunning whore of Venice / That married with Othello" (4, 2, 104–5). The final insult is tossing Emilia money as if she were the madam of a brothel.

What follows is a curious exchange. Emilia leaves and returns with Iago, who inquires as to Desdemona's state. Desdemona cannot even utter what Othello called her, but Emilia has no difficulty: "He called her 'whore'" (4, 2, 141). Iago responds to Desdemona's pain the way we would expect: with overplayed sympathy. But his lines are short, and when Desdemona asks for help, he is uncharacteristically reserved. Does something in Desdemona's plight touch him?

If we accept that Iago's prime motivation is frustrated love and that he does appreciate her qualities, then we ought to accept that he harbors affection for her. If so, he here shows a twinge of remorse, and his character becomes more complex. To be sure, the moment is transient, and when Roderigo appears, Iago resumes his familiar manner, although even that, too, seems subdued. In any case, the matter is worth speculation. With Roderigo, Iago delineates a plan to eliminate Cassio, but we intuit that Iago intends to rid himself of both men.

Left alone with Emilia, Desdemona's despair deepens, and her words and songs intimate that she expects death. In all innocence she asks:

> Dost thou in conscience think—tell me, Emilia—
> That there be women do abuse their husbands
> In such gross kind? (4, 3, 67–69)

Desdemona claims she would not behave in such a way "by this heavenly light!" (4, 3, 74), but Emilia has an answer: "Nor I neither, by this heavenly light. / I might do 't as well i' th' dark" (4, 3, 75–76). Emilia's subsequent retort reflects a cynicism about men (4, 3, 78–79) that contrasts with Desdemona's purity. The same may be said of the long speech on sexual equality (4, 3, 95–115), which seems curiously apt for our own time. Still, we wonder why Emilia does not see through her husband's deceptions.

In the next scene, while standing with Roderigo and waiting for Cassio, Iago broods on his hatred:

> If Cassio do remain,
> He hath a daily beauty in his life
> That makes me ugly. (5, 1, 18–20)

Iago is thus aware of goodness and continually works against it. Without any hope for his own advancement, he dedicates his life to creating mayhem. Once the attack against Cassio unfolds, Othello assumes that Iago has kept his promise, then hurries off to Desdemona. We know that nothing can stop him, but our feeling of helplessness grows.

After Roderigo and Cassio are each wounded in the struggle, Iago finishes Roderigo, who at last realizes what the audience has long known: "O damned Iago! O inhuman dog!" (5, 1, 74). Iago pretends to feel compassion for Cassio, then shifts blame to Bianca: "Gentlemen all, I do suspect this trash / To be a party in this injury" (5, 1, 99–100). As everyone disperses, Iago has the last word: "This is the night / That either makes me or fordoes me quite" (5, 1, 150–51). Once more we are left to ponder: Even if everything works out as he plans, what would he have?

As the final scene starts, Othello approaches the sleeping Desdemona calmly: "It is the cause, it is the cause, my soul" (5, 2, 1). He acts with cool rationality that disguises irrational passion. Yet, even as he prepares to kill, he does not want to hurt her: "Yet I'll not shed her blood, / Nor scar that whiter skin of hers than snow" (5, 2, 3–4). For the first time, we understand that he is conscious of the contrast between the colors of their skin. But when he speaks of "thy former light restore" (5, 2, 9), he clarifies that he wants to kill her, then somehow bring her back to life. He even offers her the chance to pray: "I would not kill thy unprepared spirit" (5, 2, 36).

As Othello's intention becomes clear, Desdemona vows her innocence: "I never did / Offend you in my life" (5, 2, 73–74), but as Othello recounts the circumstantial evidence against her, he is beyond reason (5, 2, 77–81). Her other dominant quality at this moment is resignation. Earlier, we admired Desdemona's independence, but here her affection for her husband leaves her looking almost angelic. Yet after she hears that Cassio has died, her expressions of sympathy arouse only further anger from Othello: "Weep'st thou for him to my face?" (5, 2, 97). Before expiring, however, she offers one last expression of loyalty: "Commend me to my kind lord" (5, 2, 153).

Given Emilia's uncertain motivations throughout the play, how ironic that she is the one who brings Othello the truth about what has happened to Cassio and Roderigo. Othello blames his own actions on Iago, but after Emilia's defense of Desdemona and the incredulous repetition of "My husband?" (5, 2, 171, 178, 182), we are reminded that had Emilia revealed the truth about the handkerchief earlier, the tragedy might have been avoided. The dramatic irony that has permeated this work is never so vivid as right here.

When Iago is brought in, Emilia, desperate to learn the truth, turns one of his choice lines back on him: "Disprove this villain, if thou be'st a man" (5, 2, 208). And when Gratiano reports Brabantio's death, Othello returns irony of his own: "'Tis pitiful" (5, 2, 250), an echo of 1, 3, 186. When Emilia is left alone with Othello, she uses her dying words to convince him: "So come my soul to bliss, as I speak true" (5, 2, 300). Only now does he see reality, and therefore he seeks another weapon by which to die.

When Gratiano returns, Othello struggles to retain his dignity as he hints at the grand adventures he has endured. Yet he continues to deceive himself about his own transgressions: "Who can control his fate?" (5, 2, 316). These words belong to someone unwilling to accept responsibility, but as Othello stares at Desdemona's lifeless body, the enormity of his crime hits him: "This look of thine will hurl my soul from heaven, / And fiends will snatch at it" (5, 2, 325–26).

Nevertheless, when Iago returns, Othello looks to Iago's feet as if to find the cloven hooves of the devil. Again he seeks to lay culpability elsewhere, for after stabbing Iago, Othello makes excuses: "An honorable murderer, if you will, / For naught I did in hate, but all in honor" (5, 2, 346–47). Even Othello sees the feebleness of this attempt at vindication, as he adds the qualifying "if you will." As in *Henry IV, Part 1* and *Julius Caesar*, honor proves the ironic cause of a man's downfall.

Iago ends fittingly: "Demand me nothing. What you know, you know. / From this time forth I never will speak word" (5, 2, 355–56). Yet what could he say, even if he wanted to confess? He has always rationalized his feelings, unable to articulate which malignancy drove him. When Lodovico asks, "What? Not to pray?" (5, 2, 357), we can imagine Iago responding with a sniff and a smirk.

After Iago is threatened with unspecified torture, the details of his plot are revealed, leaving Othello to deal with his own transgressions:

> Then you must speak
> Of one that loved not wisely, but too well;
> Of one not easily jealous, but being wrought,
> Perplexed in the extreme. (5, 2, 403–6)

Perhaps he is too charitable, but in the end he makes himself symbolically accountable for the catastrophe by taking his own life. Although Othello's final line expresses devotion to Desdemona, Lodovico best sums up the final tableau: "The object poisons sight" (5, 2, 427), uniting two dominant images of the play.

For many audiences, *Othello* is the most intimate and touching of Shakespeare's tragedies. It focuses on three characters, two of whom are happily married to each other and a third who wishes to destroy that marriage. Such destruction is not part of any larger design but carried out simply for its own sake, and the pointlessness of the violence contributes to its poignancy.

The ending of the play is also unusual, for at the conclusion of other Shakespearean tragedies, social and political order is restored. For the characters here, however, events will forever remain unknown because what happened between Othello and Iago, as well as within each one, took place before the audience alone. For us, on the other hand, the essential mystery remains: Why should innocence be made to bear such suffering?

Chapter Five

King Lear

If *Hamlet* was the play for the nineteenth century and epitomized that era's search for meaning and purpose ("To be or not to be"), *King Lear* is the play for the twentieth and twenty-first centuries, for it captures the disorder that humanity has unleashed. The play also breaks several rules of conventional dramaturgy, and although many critics believe that the script is impossible to stage properly, new productions keep appearing. In sum, within Shakespeare's canon of extraordinary works, *King Lear* may be the most extraordinary of all.

What makes it unusual? First, the plot is difficult to follow. Episodes seem to have been hurled together, an appropriate feeling for a play about chaos. After the opening scenes, the order of events is bewildering, even for audiences who have experienced them before, so be prepared to clarify for the class details of locale, motivation, and sequence, as we'll take time to do here. In addition, written and verbal communications move with unrealistic speed, so that characters accrue information that, by all rights, they should not have. Yet in the end, these unconventionalities don't matter.

Second, substantial background information is lacking. This play dramatizes the relationship between a father and three daughters, a family unit in which the mother would have been essential, but we hear nothing about such a person other than an oblique reference. Specifics about her might have clarified several puzzling issues, but all we can do is speculate. Yet the play works.

Third, the overall construction is unique. In most of Shakespeare's plays, the climax occurs in the middle of act 3. Indeed, most plays by most dramatists begin with an introduction and exposition, then move to development and complication, and continue to a climax or series of climaxes, then resolve to a dénouement. In *King Lear*, the introduction, exposition, and development are compressed into the first 120 lines of the opening scene, which should be examined virtually word for word, as we shall do. The climax occurs when Lear expels Cordelia and cedes the kingdom to Goneril and Regan. The remaining four and three-quarter acts are all resolution, the consequences of these initial actions.

Such a structure leads to a singular pattern of character development. In other Shakespearean tragedies, certain traits of the leading figure lift him or her to greatness; subsequently, under adverse conditions, those traits cause that figure to fall. But at the start of *King Lear*, we never learn whether Lear the man is great. His stature emerges strictly from his standing as king, and what causes his descent and the universal calamity that accompanies it is his abuse of greatness inherent in the kingship. Afterward, he achieves a different kind of greatness, one independent of rank.

That transformation does not come until much later, but unrest in the kingdom is apparent from Kent's opening line: "I thought the King had more affected the Duke of Albany than Cornwall" (1, 1, 1–2). He insinuates that Lear's judgment is unreliable, but we know that the position of king demands that he wield power judiciously, not impulsively. The play therefore does not portray a haphazard universe, as some characters imply, but one in which individuals are responsible for their actions. When, however, a ruler makes a decision, the entire country must deal with the aftermath.

Gloucester's response affirms these ideas:

> It did always seem so to us, but now in
> the division of the kingdom, it appears not which
> of the dukes he values most, for equalities are so
> weighed that curiosity in neither can make choice
> of either's moiety. (1, 1, 3–7)

Kent's tone suggested concern, but Gloucester's is that of a man confident that he has nothing to fear. As such, he is an analogue to Lear. Gloucester assumes that he is not vulnerable to suffering, and therefore he does not bother to distinguish between people. He is not evil, but he is thoughtless, and in this society thoughtlessness is dangerous, a lesson he will learn with unbearable viciousness.

A word about that society in general will help. Remember that the setting of this play is pre-Christian Britain, but references to Christianity dominate. Therefore we ask: Is this play Christian or not? Moreover, the mere possibility that the kingdom might be divided would have disturbed Shakespeare's audience, which had long feared the havoc that might result after the death of Queen Elizabeth. Under James I, the kingdom had stabilized, but the tension remained.

The next topic is Gloucester's illegitimate son Edmund, who stands right by him:

> His breeding, sir, hath been at my
> charge. I have so often blushed to acknowledge
> him that now I am brazed to 't. (1, 1, 9–11)

As he mocks Edmund's conception and Gloucester's own indiscretion (1, 1, 13–16), Gloucester sounds smug. He then offers kinder words about his other son, one year older and "by order of law" (1, 1, 19), but still sneers about Edmund: "There was good sport at his making, and the whoreson must be acknowledged" (1, 1, 23–24).

Gloucester's faith in "order of law" is absolute. He does not grasp that it is susceptible to ruthless forces that neither respect it nor fear it. He also jokes about the proprieties due Edgar as the older, legitimate son. In addition, Gloucester speaks casually of primogeniture (inheritance by the oldest son), a tradition that underlies the structure of his country, and again Gloucester's attitude parallels Lear's misjudgments.

With the entrance of the King, who, we later learn, is eighty years old, these themes are expanded. His first words are a command, the utterance of a man accustomed to giving orders and having them fulfilled with alacrity. Despite Kent's reservations, we have no reason to suspect that Lear does not have the loyalty of his court. His attendants offer nary a doubt, even when Lear explains his plan to divest himself of rule:

> Know that we have divided
> In three our kingdom, and 'tis our fast intent
> To shake all cares and business from our age,
> Conferring them on younger strengths, while we
> Unburdened crawl toward death. (1, 1, 39–43)

Shakespeare's audience would have been shocked by this proclamation, for by relinquishing the throne, Lear is abdicating a position regarded as divinely ordained, and by disregarding his place as the link between man and God, he threatens to disrupt the natural order. Furthermore, by partitioning the kingdom, he invites internal strife, a misjudgment that must have tragic consequences.

Next he clarifies details:

> We have this hour a constant will to publish
> Our daughters' several dowers, that future strife
> May be prevented now. (1, 1, 46–48)

These lines communicate two vital thoughts. One, Lear has already decided who will receive what, so how his daughters respond should have no bearing. Two, he is aware of antagonism among his daughters, as well as of potential conflicts over land and power. Still, he continues along this disastrous path:

> Tell me, my
> daughters—
> Since now we will divest us both of rule,

> Interest of territory, cares of state—
> Which of you shall we say doth love us most,
> That we our largest bounty may extend
> Where nature doth with merit challenge. (1, 1, 52–58)

What is he doing?

On the one hand, Lear is playing the proud father, indulging himself while trying to bring warmth to a formal occasion. On the other, he is violating the bond between parent and child. By demanding statements of love from his adult children, he treats them like participants in a performance intended to please the court and gratify his ego. His pride supersedes more important values, and when a man of such eminence permits the corruption of the royal family, results must be disastrous.

Goneril and Regan accept such humiliation stoically by offering tributes that reek of fraudulence. Goneril's is particularly ironic, for the first attribute she mentions is "eyesight" (1, 1, 62), dearer than "space" and "liberty." *Seeing* and *eyes* become major motifs, with their connotations of insight and understanding, so perhaps Goneril is subtly mocking her father's lack of such qualities.

After Lear marks Goneril's territory on the map, and as Cordelia worries how she will respond to his request, Regan answers with irony of her own: "I am made of that self mettle as my sister" (1, 1, 76), then adds, "Only she comes too short" (1, 1, 79). Her speech both flatters Lear and derogates her sister. Thus even in these few lines, we see signs of future discord.

For Cordelia, however, the situation is more difficult, and again we face a problem: Why does she not offer flattery of her own? After all, Lear clarifies that he intends to give her the largest share of the kingdom:

> Now, our joy,
> Although our last and least, to whose young love
> The vines of France and milk of Burgundy
> Strive to be interessed, what can you say to draw
> A third more opulent than your sisters'? Speak. (1, 1, 91–95)

His use of *vine* and *milk* implies that he sees Cordelia's marriage as more than a political arrangement, for it will establish the propagation of the royal line. But we notice, too, that Lear treats both of her suitors, France and Burgundy, as having an equal claim on her, and soon Burgundy shows himself much less worthy. Again, Kent's cautionary note in the opening lines proves prescient.

Cordelia's answer is simple: "Nothing, my lord" (1, 1, 96). Even after Lear repeats his question, then follows with a warning, she stands firm. Lear gives her one more chance: "Nothing will come of nothing. Speak again" (1, 1, 99). Here you should explain to the class that *nothing* has two meanings.

One is the "absence of anything," the other "chaos," and Lear implies both. Cordelia, however, remains steadfast:

> Unhappy that I am, I cannot heave
> My heart into my mouth. I love your Majesty
> According to my bond, no more nor less. (1, 1, 100–102)

She hereby shows more respect for the crown than Lear does. She also realizes the mistake of mixing the respect of a subject for a king with the love of a daughter for her father, and she is unable to compromise her integrity.

But Lear, to use the imagery of the play, is too shortsighted to appreciate her fidelity and compels her to speak further. She repeats her expression of devotion, then adds, "Why have my sisters husbands if they say / They love you all?" (1, 1, 109–10). Her logic is impeccable, for a human being may love several people without reservation. Lear, however, cannot understand such love and mistakes shared affection for divided allegiance. Over the course of the play, he learns the difference.

At this moment, though, a series of agitations have coalesced. Cordelia seems to be publicly flouting Lear's authority as father and king, as well as tarnishing what was supposed to be a majestic ritual. In addition, his favorite daughter seems to be refusing to return his love. Ironically, from our perspective, Cordelia's pride and self-assurance confirm that she is truly her father's daughter.

Then Lear asks the fatal question: "But goes thy heart with this?" (1, 1, 116), and here he reveals his lack of understanding. Cordelia has separated her father from her monarch, but Lear cannot reciprocate and has gone so far as to allow his prerogatives as king to supplant his responsibilities as father. Kingly duties can be carried out properly only when humanity is embraced, and much of the rest of the play dramatizes Lear's discovering such humanity inside himself.

Cordelia tries to redeem herself: "So young, my lord, and true" (1, 1, 119). But Lear's ego is so wounded that he completely loses perspective and shouts the climactic lines of the play:

> Then truth be thy dower, . . .
> Here I disclaim all my paternal care,
> Propinquity, and property of blood,
> And as a stranger to my heart and me
> Hold thee from this forever. (1, 1, 120–28)

In the name of all his power, both divine and temporal, he unites his bequest as father with his gift as king and expels her as daughter and subject. Furthermore, he ignores the reality that his kingdom will be left in the hands of two daughters whom he knows to be unworthy of such trust. Thus with one precipitous action, Lear shatters the order of his royal family, his government, and his nation.

When Kent tries to interject, Lear falls back on his royal station:

> Come not between the dragon and his wrath.
> I loved her most and thought to set my rest
> On her kind nursery. [*To Cordelia*] Hence and avoid
>   my sight! (1, 1, 136–39)

While summoning imagery of sight, Lear compounds his blunders by investing all authority in Goneril, Regan, and their husbands. How ironic, then, that he settles for the trappings of office: "Only we shall retain / The name and all th' addition to a king" (1, 1, 151–52). He forgets that the position must be filled by a human being.

Only Kent, who has served Lear for a long time, has the courage to oppose him:

> What wouldst thou do, old man?
> Think'st thou that duty shall have dread to speak
> When power to flattery bows? (1, 1, 163–65)

The picture of two old men raging at each other is dismaying, while the rest of Kent's speech shows that he understands Goneril and Regan as well as their capacity for mendacity. He also warns that Lear should not allow pride to overwhelm duty, but Lear is adamant and relies on intimidation instead of explanation. After he and Kent exchange accusations, invoking imagery of sight, Lear draws his sword in a caricature of masculine bravado.

The expulsion of Kent is Lear's final expression of temper (1, 1, 191–203), and Kent's touching farewell to Cordelia and his cold words to her sisters earn no response from Goneril and Regan. They have what they want. Kent's warning is also meant for Lear, but Lear has never disagreed with Kent's judgment, only his propriety. Lear believes that his power justifies his actions, but he forgets that the proper exercise of power demands responsibility.

One counterpart to Lear is the Duke of France, brought in as a prospect for Cordelia's hand in marriage. After Burgundy rejects her because she has lost her inheritance, France speaks:

> Sure her offense
> Must be of such unnatural degree
> That monsters it, or your forevouched affection
> Fall into taint. (1, 1, 251–54)

His use of *unnatural* suggests opposing nature or the natural scheme of things, but in fact Lear has acted unnaturally by ripping apart his family and kingdom and unleashing the "monster" that becomes a theme of this play. In Lear's terrifying words, "Better thou / Hadst not been born than not t' have pleased me better" (1, 1, 269–70).

Lear responds to France's challenge with a fitting reply: "Nothing. I have sworn. I am firm" (1, 1, 283). He imagines that he is being ironic, but the irony will turn back on him. Cordelia then leaves her sisters with bitter parting: "I know what you are" (1, 1, 312), but they remain unmoved, and when the two are left alone, Goneril clarifies what we know:

> He always loved our sister most, and with
> what poor judgment he hath now cast her off
> appears too grossly. (1, 1, 336–38)

We never learn which forces have shaped these women. All they know is that they hate their father and sister and are content to base their actions on that hate. Because they never try to understand themselves, they eliminate possibility of redemption.

Such uncertainty is not the case with Edmund, who manifests forces that would take advantage of errors like those Lear has committed: "Thou, Nature, art my goddess. To thy law / My services are bound" (1, 2, 1–2). This nature is not the benign order to which France referred or the individual temperament Lear described but a brutal law of the jungle. Edmund is another Machiavel (for further discussion, check the analysis of Iago in *Othello* in chapter 4), but unlike Iago, Edmund understands his motives. He wants his father's wealth:

> Wherefore should I
> Stand in the plague of custom, and permit
> The curiosity of nations to deprive me
> For that I am some twelve or fourteen moonshines
> Lag of a brother? (1, 2, 2–7)

He refuses to accept the values of a society that rejects him, and in 1, 2, 12–15, he praises the energy with which he was conceived as evidence of his superiority.

Edmund claims: "I grow, I prosper. / Now, gods, stand up for bastards!" (1, 2, 22–23). Here is the formidable danger that in this play confronts goodness, as embodied first by Kent and Cordelia and later by Edgar, the Fool, and Albany. In opposition are Goneril, Regan, Edmund, Cornwall, and later Oswald. Good battles evil for possession of the world. Good survives but at a frightful cost, and the meaning of that survival is not clear.

At the center of the struggle are two aging men. The first scene revealed Lear's flaws and how they led him astray. This scene shows Gloucester's undoing, and the similarity to Lear is suggested by Gloucester's words. For instance, in response to Edmund's answer about what he is hiding, "Nothing, my lord" (1, 2, 33), Gloucester replies with Lear's self-satisfaction: "The quality of nothing hath not such need to hide itself" (1, 2, 35–36). He then accepts from Edmund a letter supposedly written by Edgar, and which implies that Edgar plans to commit treason.

Gloucester's response is to look to the heavens: "These late eclipses in the sun and moon portend no good to us" (1, 2, 109–10). But why does he believe Edmund? Why does he not ask Edgar? Like Lear, he misjudges his children, then refuses to acknowledge the possibility of his own misjudgment, as Edmund later clarifies:

> This is the excellent foppery of the world, that
> when we are sick in fortune (often the surfeits of
> our own behavior) we make guilty of our disasters
> the sun, the moon, and stars. (1, 2, 125–28)

Edmund's reliance on his will reflects a refusal to be bound by moral restraint. As he observes later: "Let me, if not by birth, have lands by wit" (1, 2, 191).

The next scene shows the beginnings of the chaos that Lear has unleashed. We have little sympathy for Goneril but understand as she complains to her servant, Oswald: "His knights grow riotous, and himself upbraids us / On every trifle" (1, 3, 7–8). What she sees is not corruption caused by abuse of power but the danger of a vacuum of power. Thus her long-concealed antagonism toward Lear may be released without fear of retribution.

After a disguised Kent returns to offer his services to Lear (under the name Caius, as we eventually learn), the king seems pleased but still calls for his Fool. Eventually a knight reports: "Since my young lady's going into France, sir, the Fool hath much pined away" (1, 4, 73–74). The affection of the Fool for Cordelia is important, for he is in many respects her surrogate. The two never appear together, and according to tradition, they were played by the same actor. In any case, the Fool is Lear's conscience outside civilization, while Cordelia fulfills that role within society.

When the Fool arrives, he begins to exercise his right to say what others may not. Much of the Fool's language is difficult to grasp, but certain themes emerge. The passage about the cloving of the egg, for instance, suggests that it is a symbol of fertility for the kingdom and the family. Lear understands the intimation: "Dost thou call me 'fool,' boy?" (1, 4, 152). The Fool always has a ready answer: "All thy other titles thou hast given away. That thou wast born with" (1, 4, 153–54). And a moment later: "Thou hadst little wit in thy bald crown when they gav'st thy golden one away" (1, 4, 166–67).

When Goneril enters to berate her father over the intemperate actions of his troops (1, 4, 206–19), Lear is already confused: "Who is it that can tell me who I am?" (1, 4, 236). Only the Fool dares do so: "Lear's shadow" (1, 4, 237). *Shadow* also has connotations of homosexuality, so perhaps the Fool is implying that by surrendering the throne, Lear has emasculated himself.

Goneril continues her tirade (1, 4, 244–59), forcing Lear to a terrible realization: "O most small fault, / How ugly didst thou in Cordelia show" (1,

4, 278–79). For a man who exercises authority, even a slight error may have grave results, and in a rare stage direction, Shakespeare writes that Lear "*strikes his head*" (1, 4, 283). Soon he turns his anger on Goneril:

> Hear, Nature, hear, dear goddess, hear!
> Suspend thy purpose if thou didst intend
> To make this creature fruitful. (1, 4, 289–91)

Perhaps needless to say, this "goddess" is very different from Edmund's (1, 2, 1). Yet the ferocity of Lear's execration is undercut by its ineffectuality, as well as his ill-considered intention to find relief at the home of Regan (1, 4, 322–23), where Goneril sends Oswald to warn of Lear's arrival.

Amid increasing animal imagery in this scene, the only leavening element is Albany, whose brief lines hint at an incipient conscience within him. Goneril mocks her husband for "This milky gentleness" (1, 4, 364), insinuating effeminacy, but Albany does not back down: "How far your eyes may pierce I cannot tell. / Striving to better, oft we mar what's well" (1, 4, 368–69). Meanwhile Lear battles on: "O, let me not be mad, not mad, sweet heaven!" (1, 5, 45). He will never surrender.

In act 2, events hurtle forward as consequences of Lear's actions begin to take hold. At Gloucester's castle, Edmund learns that war has broken out between Albany and Cornwall. To further his own ends, Edmund begins a mock duel with Edgar, then uses a self-inflicted wound to confirm Gloucester's fears about his older son (2, 1, 36–38). At that point Cornwall and Regan, having left their own home to avoid Lear, offer mock sympathy to Gloucester and invite Edmund to join them (2, 1, 129–35). All these events suggest that the forces of malevolence are consolidating, but one theme of this play is that inevitably they will turn on one another.

When Kent arrives, he tangles with Oswald, a brave act but also a foolhardy one, for Kent is in enemy territory. Even before his superiors, Kent is fearless:

> I have seen better faces in my time
> Than stands on any shoulder that I see
> Before me at this instant. (2, 2, 97–99)

His reward for such effrontery is the order from Cornwall that Kent be put in the stocks until noon, but Regan extends the punishment: "Till noon? Till night, my lord, and all night, too" (2, 2, 147). Given Kent's age and position with Lear, such treatment is a gross insult, but Gloucester is helpless to protest (2, 2, 153–60).

Left alone, Kent ruminates over a letter from Cordelia, which has arrived with startling speed. He also resolves that in spite of his suffering, he will endure: "Fortune, good night. Smile once more; turn thy wheel" (2, 2, 188–89). The image of the wheel, popular in Shakespeare's day, reflects the belief that the nature Lear holds sacred will eventually triumph. Whether such trust is justified and whether the world Shakespeare dramatizes is ultimately benign is one of the key issues of the play.

Another strategy is followed by Edgar, who appears before us to seek anonymity as Poor Tom, a madman: "And with presented nakedness outface / The winds and persecutions of the sky" (2, 3, 11–12). He also hopes to escape persecution from human society. That role, however, also anticipates the upcoming crisis endured by Lear, as Edgar hints: "'Edgar' I nothing am" (2, 3, 21).

When Lear arrives at Gloucester's castle, he is outraged to see his man in the stocks: "They durst not do 't. / They could not, would not do 't" (2, 4, 25–26). But when he moves inside to find Regan, their refusal to meet with him compounds his frustration: "Deny to speak with me? They are sick? They are weary?" (2, 4, 94–95). Gloucester tries to comfort Lear by apologizing for Cornwall: "How unremovable and fixed he is / In his own course" (2, 4, 101–2). We recognize, though, that Gloucester is unintentionally describing Lear's attitude in the first scene of the play.

Despite his rage, Lear still understands the dynamics of a world turned upside down:

> We are not ourselves
> When nature, being oppressed, commands the mind
> To suffer with the body. I'll forbear. (2, 4, 120–22)

We see signs of self-awareness, as well as resolve to fight. Thus when Regan enters with a polite but casual greeting: "I am glad to see your Highness" (2, 4, 143), Lear responds with acid irony: "if thou shouldst not be glad, / I would divorce me from thy mother's tomb" (2, 4, 145–46). This rare mention of Lear's wife leads us to theorize about her. Given that Cordelia resembles her father and that Regan and Goneril both differ so profoundly from their sister, we may conclude that the two older daughters inherited their attitude and values from their mother.

One way Regan differs from Goneril, however, is that Regan offers her father false solace:

> O sir, you are old.
> Nature in you stands on the very verge
> Of his confine. You should be ruled and led
> By some discretion that discerns your state
> Better than you yourself. Therefore, I pray you
> That to our sister you do make return.
> Say you have wronged her. (2, 4, 164–70)

In his fury, Lear fails to understand that Regan is just as cruel as her sister: "Her eyes are fierce, but thine / Do comfort and not burn" (2, 4, 194–96). He adds, "Thou better know'st / The offices of nature, bond of childhood" (2, 4,

200–201). He forgets that he inflicted similar humiliation on Cordelia. Yet even though he has been wrong, his debasement is excruciating to witness.

He better understands his plight when Goneril enters, and her alliance with Regan becomes apparent. Cornwall admits that he put Kent in the stocks, but when Regan augments the insult by suggesting that Lear dismiss half his troops, his reaction is ferocious:

> But yet thou art my flesh, my blood, my daughter,
> Or, rather, a disease that's in my flesh,
> Which I must needs call mine. (2, 4, 254–56)

Even as he disowns her, Lear acknowledges that he is the origin of this evil, both the biological father and the ruler who unleashed it. He also continues to abandon the royal "we" and speaks in first person singular.

From this point on, the sisters toy with him unmercifully, inquiring why he needs any train at all. Lear attempts to fight back: "I gave you all—" (2, 4, 286), but Regan interrupts, "And in good time you gave it" (2, 4, 287). She reminds him that they were not his first choice. Now Lear begins to find his humanity:

> O, reason not the need! Our basest beggars
> Are in the poorest thing superfluous.
> Allow not nature more than nature needs,
> Man's life is cheap as beast's. (2, 4, 304–7)

He attempts to explain human pride and dignity, qualities that in the first scene he ignored.

As he regards himself more as man than king, he raises the question that pervades the rest of the play:

> You see me here, you gods, a poor old man
> As full of grief as age, wretched in both.
> If it be you that stirs these daughters' hearts
> Against their father, fool me not so much
> To bear it tamely. (2, 4, 313–17)

He poses the greatest conundrum of all: What kind of a world allows such evil to run rampant? The rest of this speech (2, 4, 317–27) is a blend of anger and valor, but Lear is so possessed by fury that he cannot articulate his thoughts, and abdication has left him no means of revenge. Meanwhile, the storm outside reflects two others: the turmoil in the kingdom and the one in Lear's mind. After Lear is expelled, Goneril finally places responsibility on the King himself: "'Tis his own blame put himself from rest, / And must needs taste his folly" (2, 4, 331–32).

While the storm continues with "eyeless rage" (3, 1, 9), as a gentleman confirms, Kent has news of his own. Dissension between Albany and Cornwall is creating civil war, another consequence of Lear's misjudgment.

Meanwhile, France is preparing to invade England, a circumstance that would have put Shakespeare's audience in the odd position of supporting the forces of a foreign country against those of England. How such information moved so quickly is never clarified.

The next scene is too large for any stage to encompass. Defenseless in the middle of the storm, Lear bellows against the heavens in a tone both magnificent and fearsome: "I never gave you kingdom, called you children; / You owe me no subscription. . . . But yet I call you servile ministers" (3, 2, 19–20, 23). No matter how harshly nature batters Lear, it can never be as cruel as his daughters. Such a moment emphasizes man's smallness against the great expanse of the universe but also brings out man's potential dignity.

For the first time, Lear grapples with his plight: "I am a man / More sinned against than sinning" (3, 2, 62–63). He also evinces a new humanity, as he speaks to the Fool:

> Where is this straw, my fellow?
> The art of our necessities is strange
> And can make vile things precious. (3, 2, 75–77)

(If time permits, one film excerpt to show the class is the storm scene from Peter Brook's film of the play, starring Paul Scofield. The dizzying camera shots and the drenching rain communicate the madness of Lear's world as well as any performance can.)

When Gloucester comments on "unnatural dealing," (3, 3, 2), then reveals to Edmund that plans to aid Lear are taking shape, we cringe at the old man's confiding in someone we know to be corrupt. Even worse is Gloucester's revealing that an attack is coming from France (3, 3, 12–14), and the son's response encapsulates much of the play: "The younger rises when the old doth fall" (3, 3, 25).

Lear, Kent, and the Fool find comfort in a hovel, where Lear broods on the fate of "Poor naked wretches" (3, 4, 32). Until now, he has given them scarcely a thought, but now his perspective has changed:

> Take physic, pomp.
> Expose thyself to feel what wretches feel,
> That thou may'st shake the superflux to them
> And show the heavens more just. (3, 3, 38–41)

The moment is wondrous. A king who has enjoyed absolute power realizes that his rule has been misguided. Can we doubt that were he to regain his throne, he would be a wiser, more compassionate king? Here is one place where the play may be considered hopeful.

When Edgar, disguised as Poor Tom, emerges from the hovel, Lear suggests the reason for the intruder's madness: "Has his daughters brought him to this pass?— / Couldst thou save nothing? Wouldst thou give 'em all?" (3, 4, 68–70). As the dialogue overflows with bizarre images and obscure, sometimes impenetrable references, we are confronted by a fantastic trio: Lear, on the edge of madness; Tom, feigning madness; and the fool, whose recondite wit borders on madness.

Looking at Tom, Lear recognizes man's puniness:

> Thou art the thing itself; unaccomodated
> man is no more but such a poor, bare,
> forked animal as thou art. (3, 4, 113–15)

In sympathy with Tom, Lear begins to tear off his clothes, and when Gloucester somehow finds this place of refuge, his regrets add to the general disorder, for he does not recognize his own child:

> I am almost mad myself. I had a son,
> Now outlawed from my blood. He sought my life
> But lately, very late. I loved him, friend,
> No father his son dearer. (3, 4, 176–79)

The impossible odds that oppose these lost souls is apparent when Cornwall and Edmund resolve to work together. The former believes the lies about Edgar that Edmund has told and as reward names Edmund Earl of Gloucester. The scene borders on the blasphemous, as the pair bandy about words like *loyalty* (3, 5, 4), *just* (3, 5, 11), *trust* (3, 5, 25), and *love* (3, 5, 26), all the while trafficking in deception and hate.

The movement between locales takes us back to the hovel, where Lear and the Fool carry on a mock trial of Goneril and Regan. As Lear interrogates a stool that stands for Goneril, Edgar can barely contain himself: "My tears begin to take his part so much / They mar my counterfeiting" (3, 6, 63–64). Lear finally poses the question that dominates the play:

> Then let them anatomize Regan; see what breeds
> about her heart. Is there any cause in nature that
> makes these hard hearts? (3, 6, 80–82)

In a benign universe, how can such figures as Goneril and Regan prevail? No answer is forthcoming. Not long after, the Fool offers his final words of the play: "And I'll go to bed at noon" (3, 6, 90). The line has intimations of death, and from this point forward the word *fool*, which has denotations of both "clown" and "one held in affection," seems to apply to the Fool and Cordelia alike.

Gloucester returns to warn that Lear's life is in danger, as is the life of anyone found with him, and urges that Lear be taken to Dover (3, 6, 101–3). In the scene to follow, Gloucester's solicitude proves tragically ironic. Edgar is almost too stunned to act: "When we our betters see bearing our woes, / We scarcely think our miseries our foes" (3, 6, 111–12). He, too, ponders the fundamental injustice in the world.

The next scene is perhaps the most unbearable in dramatic literature. Cornwall writes to Albany, hoping that in the face of a French attack, the two sides may unite. He then summons Gloucester, now judged a traitor. As the sisters advocate swift and violent punishment, Cornwall chooses to decide for himself but first asks Edmund to depart. That Edmund calmly does so, leaving his father at the mercy of three fiends, tells us all we need to know about Edmund.

Bound to the chair, Gloucester endures their sadistic charade. In Regan's words: "Be simple-answered, for we know the truth" (3, 7, 52). Gloucester speaks up bravely: "Because I would not see thy cruel nails / Pluck out his poor old eyes" (3, 7, 69–70). But he anticipates his own torture, when Cornwall tears out one of the old man's eyes. Even at this horrible moment, goodness persists, as a servant stabs Cornwall. Regan kills the rebel, but a measure of hope survives.

After Cornwall brutally tears out the other eye, Gloucester in agony cries for Edmund, but Regan answers, "It was he / That made the overture of thy treasons to us" (3, 7, 108–9). At last Gloucester "sees" the truth: "O my follies! Then Edgar was abused. / Kind gods, forgive me that, and prosper him" (3, 7, 111–12). We remember Edmund's early soliloquy: "I grow. I prosper" (1, 2, 22). The determination shown by the servants provides one more bit of hope: "I'll never care what wickedness I do / If this man come to good" (3, 7, 120–21). That man's confidence will be restored, as will this one's:

> If she live long
> And in the end meet the old course of death,
> Women will all turn monsters. (3, 7, 122–24)

He anticipates Regan's death, but we note that women have already turned "monsters."

Gloucester's misery continues when he meets an old man on the road and tells him: "I have no way and therefore want no eyes. / I stumbled when I saw" (4, 1, 19–20). Gloucester then pronounces his affection for Edgar (4, 1, 20–25), who was perhaps always on Gloucester's mind during his earlier encounter with Poor Tom. Now, though, pessimism overwhelms the sightless man: "As flies to wanton boys are we to th' gods; / They kill us for their sport" (4, 1, 41–42).

In 1, 2, Gloucester spoke of the stars determining human action, and in 3, 7, he acknowledged his own responsibility. Now, bereft of faith, he speaks of a random, meaningless universe. Some audiences take this statement as reflecting Shakespeare's values, but the remainder of the work has positive moments that clarify that this attitude is the personal vision of the character Gloucester, not of the playwright.

When Edgar speaks and steps forward, his voice sparks a bit of remembrance in Gloucester, who remembers him as Poor Tom but not as Edgar. As they leave for Dover, Gloucester sounds a different assessment:

> Let the superfluous and lust-dieted man,
> That slaves your ordinance, that will not see
> Because he does not feel, feel your power quickly. (4, 1, 77–79)

Gloucester accepts his own punishment but hopes that others whom he judges to be guiltier will also suffer.

Oswald reports about Albany's turning away from Goneril, but she dismisses such action as the result of Albany's "cowish terror of his spirit" (4, 2, 15). Besides, she is more interested in Edmund, with whom she shares a kiss before he departs with characteristic gallantry: "Yours in the ranks of death" (4, 2, 30). Albany then arrives to provide a moral upsurge, as he lambasts Goneril and Regan in appropriately animalistic terms, then expresses hope that justice might prevail:

> If that the heavens do not their visible spirits
> Send quickly down to tame these vile offenses.
> It will come:
> Humanity must perforce prey on itself,
> Like monsters of the deep. (4, 2, 57–61)

A servant's report about Cornwall's death suggests that Albany's call is being answered, but the concomitant news that Gloucester has been blinded shocks Albany. Goneril, however, worries that Edmund may link up with the widowed Regan and therefore retreats to plan strategy. We feel that balance of power slowly shifting from evil to good.

Now the military campaign about which we have heard comes to the fore. Because Cordelia leads the French forces (4, 3, 1–7), Shakespeare's audience would have difficulty supporting her, but the gentlemen describes her in terms that seem borrowed from Albany:

> There she shook
> The holy water from her heavenly eyes,
> And clamor moistened. (4, 3, 34–36)

Kent then ponders why she should be vastly different from her sisters: "It is the stars. / The stars above us govern our conditions" (4, 3, 38–39). Kent is admirable and courageous, but Shakespeare's plays dramatize again and again that responsibility lies not with the supernatural but with humanity.

The long-awaited reunion between Cordelia and Lear is linked with military action that supports it. The doctor comments on the means for Lear's recovery: "Our foster nurse of nature is repose / The which he lacks" (4, 4, 13–14). Here is another aspect of the beneficent qualities of nature. Cordelia then adds a political note: "O dear father, / It is thy business that I go about"

(4, 4, 26–27). Her goal is the restoration of a legitimate king to the English throne, and thus the English audience advocates her cause.

The next scene shows us evil turning further on itself. While Albany is caught between fealty to the rulers of his country and his desire to protect Lear and Cordelia, Regan's suspicions about Goneril's lust for Edmund have increased. As Regan says to Oswald, "I know your lady does not love her husband" (4, 5, 27). She then asks Oswald for the letter that Goneril has written to Edmund, simultaneously inviting Oswald to deliver a letter of her own. For his part, Oswald appears willing to shift sides in the hope of eventually aligning himself with the winner (4, 5, 43–44). His treachery befits both of the women for whom he works.

The next scene presents a challenge. As Edgar leads his blind father, Gloucester imagines that he approaches the cliffs at Dover. He even thinks he recognizes his son's voice. Whereas once he could not see a reality that destroyed him, now he imagines a fantasy that will save him. As he stands before what he envisions to be a cliff, he reconciles himself to suicide: "This world I do renounce, and in your sights / Shake patiently my great affliction off" (4, 6, 45–46). And when he jumps, the moment of resignation illuminates Lear's refusal to capitulate.

This action must be carefully staged, for Gloucester topples forward as if from a high cliff but in fact drops only a foot or so. Thus anticlimactic laughter must be avoided. When Gloucester awakens, Edgar pretends to be a stranger who believes Gloucester's surviving such a fall to be a miracle (4, 6, 69). Edgar then adds:

> Therefore, thou happy father,
> Think that the clearest gods, who make them
>   honors,
> Of men's impossibilities, have preserved thee. (4, 6, 89–92)

Gloucester is convinced and vows to hold onto life as long as he can endure (4, 6, 93–95).

Such optimism is undercut immediately by the entrance of Lear, bedecked madly in flowers. As he barks commands to imaginary courtiers, Gloucester recognizes Lear's voice, to which the king replies, "Ay, every inch a king" (4, 6, 126). His endurance is overwhelming, but his ravings mirror the discord into which his world has collapsed, especially as he exhorts against female sexuality (4, 6, 130–42). When Gloucester asks to kiss his hand, Lear's reply reflects new recognition: "Let me wipe it first; it smells of mortality" (4, 6, 148). He then embarks on a litany of corruptions in which the powerful are as guilty as those they punish (4, 6, 175–90).

This scene between these two distraught men raving about the universe climaxes with Lear's reflections on life: "When we are born, we cry that we are come / To this great stage of fools" (4, 6, 200–201). The image of human being as actor is, not surprisingly, a familiar one for Shakespeare. You might remind the class of Jaques's "All the world's a stage" from *As You Like It* (2, 7, 146–73); Macbeth's "Life's but a walking shadow, a poor player" from *Macbeth* (5, 5, 27–31); and Prospero's "These our actors" from *The Tempest* (4, 1, 165–75).

Throughout this scene, Lear alternates between two perspectives: One, the world is corrupt and meaningless, and two, humanity is responsible for its condition. When the Gentlemen mentions Cordelia, he suggests that the latter interpretation is correct:

> Thou hast a daughter
> Who redeems nature from the general curse
> Which twain have brought her to. (4, 6, 225–27)

His words echo the sentiments of Albany (4, 2, 57–61), and after this expression of hope, Gloucester himself is moved to exclaim:

> You ever-gentle gods, take my breath from me;
> Let not my worser spirit tempt me again
> To die before you please. (4, 6, 241–43)

Here Oswald enters prepared to kill Gloucester, but Edgar, still as Tom, intervenes and slays Oswald. With his dying words, Oswald begs that the letter he carries be given to Edmund. Oswald's allegiance remains with Goneril, as Edgar discovers by reading the letter. He also understands Edmund's duplicity, as well as Albany's steadfastness (4, 6, 301–2). We feel humanity's benevolence slowly overcoming widespread injustice.

The long-awaited reconciliation occurs in the next scene. First Cordelia and Kent exchange expressions of gratitude, and her willingness to maintain his other identity contrasts with the treachery practiced by others. When the doctor explains that Lear still sleeps, Cordelia expresses her faith: "O, you kind gods, / Cure this great breach in his abusèd nature!" (4, 7, 16–17). Such a vision clashes with the nihilistic sentiments of others. Finally, as Cordelia gazes at her father, she ponders the miracle before her: "'Tis wonder that thy life and wits at once / Had not concluded all" (4, 7, 47–48).

When Lear wakes, he sees Cordelia's face and assumes she is an angel: "You are a spirit, I know. Where did you die?" (4, 7, 56). We remember Albany's comment about "visible spirits" (4, 2, 57). As he gains awareness, Lear's language remains humble and unaffected:

> I am a very foolish fond old man,
> Fourscore and upward, not an hour more nor less,
> And to deal plainly,
> I fear I am not in my perfect mind. (4, 7, 69–72)

After he recognizes her, he begs forgiveness:

> I know you do not love me, for your sisters

> Have, as I do remember, done me wrong.
> You have some cause; they have not. (4, 7, 83–85)

The simplicity of her next line makes it the most touching of the play: "No cause, no cause" (4, 7, 85–86). Then Kent assures Lear of his royalty: "In your own kingdom, sir" (4, 7, 89). The scene concludes with word of the death of Cornwall and Edmund's leading the English forces. The battle is almost underway.

In the next scene, the opposition takes center stage. Edmund again questions Albany's loyalty, but Regan is more absorbed with whether Edmund has slept with Goneril (5, 1, 12–13). Her curiosity amuses Edmund: "That thought abuses you" (5, 1, 14), but when Goneril enters with Albany, she shows the same concern as Regan: "I had rather lose the battle than that sister / Should loosen him and me" (5, 1, 21–22). Albany, however, has his own priorities:

> It touches us as France invades our land,
> Not bolds the King, with others whom, I fear,
> Most just and heavy causes make oppose. (5, 1, 28–30)

In contrast to the selfishness of the two sisters and Edmund, Albany worries most about his country.

As the battle draws nearer, Edgar, in disguise as a peasant, brings Goneril's treacherous letter for Albany. He, however, seems to have no time to read it and gives it to Edmund, who peruses it, then reflects on his choice between two sisters: "Neither can be enjoyed / If both remain alive" (5, 1, 66–67), and he assumes that one of them will kill Albany (5, 1, 70–73). More deadly, however, is his scheme to kill Cordelia and Lear: "The battle done and they within our power, / Shall never see his pardon" (5, 1, 75–76). At this point, Shakespeare has us wondering just how brutal the end of this play will be.

The next scene dramatizes how the war has progressed. Edgar shields Gloucester, but the army of Cordelia is defeated, and she and Lear are captured. Edgar handles that news as best he can:

> Men must endure
> Their going hence even as their coming hither.
> Ripeness is all. (5, 2, 10–12)

That last line suggests that no matter which external forces influence a human life, individual strength and understanding give meaning to that life. This attitude prepares us for the final scene, when the question of such purpose is thrust before us once more.

As that scene begins, Cordelia and Lear are brought in as prisoners, and her words reflect her resolve: "We are not the first / Who with best meaning have incurred the worst" (5, 3, 4–5). Lear rejects all possibilities of unifying the royal family: "No, no, no, no. Come, let's away to prison. / We two alone will sing like birds i' th' cage" (5, 3, 9–10). He also understands the transience of worldly power: "who's in, who's out" (5, 3, 16), and that political leaders come and go: "packs and sects of great ones / That ebb and flow by th' moon" (5, 3, 19–20). At Edmund's command, the two are taken away, with Lear ever bold: "We'll see 'em starved first" (5, 3, 28–29).

Edmund adheres to his personal code by giving his Captain a letter that orders the execution of Lear and Cordelia, but he is challenged by the entrance of Albany, who demands Edmund's captives. Edmund defends his securing of Lear by suggesting that the presence of the King might incite rebellion among their own troops (5, 3, 52–59), but Albany dismisses this explanation by denouncing Edmund as a lesser officer (5, 3, 68–70). Regan and Goneril speak up on Edmund's behalf, and even Regan's sudden illness does not diminish her devotion to him: "Witness the world I create thee here/ My lord and master" (5, 3, 91–92).

Her sister's discomfort inspires Goneril's mockery: "Mean you to enjoy him?" (5, 3, 93), and we immediately suspect Goneril is responsible for Regan's condition. As Edmund attempts to assert his will (5, 3, 95), Albany accuses him of treason, and we realize that Albany must have read Goneril's letter and now knows of the feelings among both women and Edmund. Following Edgar's earlier instructions (5, 1, 55), Albany throws down his glove to challenge Edmund, who boldly accepts, as Regan is carried away.

The Herald's call is answered by a disguised Edgar, and again we feel the forces of justice taking control. Edgar accuses Edmund, "thou art a traitor, / False to thy gods, thy brother, and thy father" (5, 3, 161–62). We understand, however, that Edmund has in fact been loyal to his god, the law of the jungle. During the fight Edmund is wounded, and Albany orders him saved, no doubt for trial. Goneril speaks out on Edmund's behalf, but Albany pulls out her letter: "Thou worse than any name, read thine own evil" (5, 3, 187). Even after she strides off, Albany orders that she be guarded, again for likely trial.

Edmund's fatal wound brings out another side of him: "What you have charged me with, that have I done, / And more, much more" (5, 3, 195–96). To what does he refer? And if he is repenting, why does he not halt the executions of Lear and Cordelia? No answer is forthcoming, and only Edgar speaks, first identifying himself, then asserting his view of a fair world: "The gods are just, and of our pleasant vices / Make instruments to plague us" (5, 3, 204–5). Even Edmund agrees: "The wheel is come full circle; I am here" (5, 3, 209).

Edgar relates about hiding Gloucester and how the revelation that Tom o' Bedlam was his son was too much for the old man, whose heart: "'Twixt two extremes of passion, joy and grief, / Burst smilingly" (5, 3, 234–35). Gloucester's offstage death will make Lear's that much more dramatic. At last Edmund seems to reconcile himself with his brother: "This speech of yours hath moved me" (5, 3, 236). The line implies that Edmund's pardon of Lear is forthcoming, but Shakespeare again postpones it, almost taunting the audience, while Edmund furnishes additional information about his past.

The subsequent deaths of Goneril and Regan provoke only his wit: "I was contracted to them both. All three / Now marry in an instant" (5, 3, 270–71). And when Kent arrives to inquire about Lear, Edmund offers one more bitter reflection:

> Yet Edmund was beloved.
> The one the other poisoned for my sake,
> And after slew herself. (5, 3, 287–89)

At last he is inspired to revoke the writ of execution on Lear and Cordelia (5, 3, 291–95), so again we believe that the worst might be avoided.

Instead, what follows is the most shattering scene in a play filled with them, as Lear enters carrying the body of the dead Cordelia. The great critic and lexicographer Samuel Johnson (1709–1784) found this scene unbearable and was unable to read the play because of it. For roughly a century and a half, a revised version (1681) by poet Nahum Tate (1652–1715) held sway, in which Lear is restored to his throne and Cordelia marries Edgar. Today, however, we are left with Shakespeare's devastating conclusion.

Is it appropriate? So much of the play has moved toward the reestablishment of justice, and the death of Cordelia serves no purpose. But that very pointlessness is essential to the ending, for it returns us to the mystery of existence, the core question of this play and of Shakespearean tragedy. Does the death of Cordelia suggest a random universe?

Much of the rest of the conclusion implies otherwise. Lear desperately maintains hope that Cordelia may live (5, 3, 313–15), while Kent muses in dejection: "Is this the promised end?" (5, 3, 316). He intimates that after this tragedy, nothing can have meaning. Lear, however, hopes that if Cordelia breathes, she will redeem others (5, 3, 319–21). Is Cordelia therefore a Christ figure who dies for the sins of others? Lear also reveals that he killed the man who tried to hang Cordelia (5, 3, 330), and we are asked to believe that a man of eighty would be able to summon such strength. Lear then recognizes Kent but does not realize that Kent and Caius are the same.

Even word that his other daughters have died means nothing to Lear, and the report about Edmund's expiring is dismissed by Albany, who nobly abdicates the throne so that Lear may resume his place. The King, however, is too preoccupied to care. Instead he mourns: "And my poor fool is hanged" (5, 3, 369). Whether he refers to Cordelia or his own Fool is unclear, but the blending of the two is proper.

Then Lear asks the most daunting question of all: "Why should a dog, a horse, a rat have life, / And thou no breath at all?" (5, 3, 370–71). Why does suffering exist in the world? The play provides no answer. The finality of his words, though, is stunning: "Thou'lt come no more, / Never, never, never, never, never" (5, 3, 371–72). After modestly asking for someone to undo his button, Lear suddenly imagines that Cordelia breathes again, but the excitement is too great, and he dies. Whether he does so because of happiness or a broken heart is one more uncertainty.

Albany begins the restoration of order by offering the crown to Kent and Edgar, but Kent demurs: "I have a journey, sir, shortly to go; / My master calls me. I must not say no" (5, 3, 390–91). He anticipates joining Lear in death, leaving Edgar to bring events to their conclusion: "The oldest hath borne most; we that are young / Shall never see so much nor live so long" (5, 3, 394–95). His hope is that Lear's life has taught others who will follow.

King Lear is in many ways the most overwhelming work, not only by Shakespeare, but also by any dramatist. Its prodigious roster of characters encompasses the range of humanity, and the heights of love and depths of hate are almost too much to assimilate. Yet the work does have thematic unity. No matter how much suffering we endure, no matter how unfathomable the mysteries of the universe might be, the capacity of the human heart to learn and forgive redeems us.

Chapter Six

Macbeth

This play has traditionally been regarded as ill-fated, primarily because so many productions have gone awry. One legend is that on opening night the original Lady Macbeth became sick, and Shakespeare himself took the part. Over the centuries, numerous actors, directors, producers, stagehands, family members, friends, and even audience members have suffered injuries, fallen ill, or been killed during a run, and many performances have received particularly harsh reviews.

As a result, even mentioning the title is considered bad form, and theater folk instead refer to it as the "Scottish Play" and the two lead characters as the "Scottish king" and the "Scottish queen." Indeed, to pronounce the real title in an actual theater (outside of performance) or to quote lines from the text anywhere on the premises is to invite disaster, so the offending party is required to leave the building, spin three times, curse, spit, and then knock to gain readmittance.

Why should the play have such a history? Superstitious people claim that in the scenes with the witches Shakespeare included legitimate incantations that have forever marked the work. On a more practical level, because much of the action occurs at night and therefore the lighting must be dim, numerous fights and other exertions that the script demands invite mishap. Whatever the reason, informing students that they are venturing into risky territory should provoke interest.

Shakespeare's source is Holinshed's *Chronicles of England, Scotland, and Ireland*, which also provided background for his history plays. In adapting this material, however, Shakespeare made several important changes. In Holinshed, Macbeth has a legitimate grievance against a young and incompetent King Duncan, but in the play Duncan is older and decent, and Macbeth's motivation is not political. Next, Shakespeare dispenses with what Holinshed describes as a successful ten-year reign for Macbeth and turns him into a tyrant who rules briefly and cruelly.

Finally, in Holinshed Banquo is Macbeth's accomplice, but in Shakespeare's play Banquo is a noble bystander, probably because he was a forbear of King James, formerly king of Scotland, who succeeded to the English throne in 1603 after the death of Queen Elizabeth. James was a student of witchcraft and demonology and even wrote a book on the subject. Therefore the play may be understood as a tribute to him and his deep interest in Scottish history. We should also note that given the depth of Lady Macbeth's character, Shakespeare must have felt that he finally had a young male actor capable of handling such a daunting role.

The result of these alterations is emphasis not on political ramifications, as in Holinshed, but on psychological and moral implications. *Macbeth* is also the shortest of Shakespeare's tragedies, and scholars have surmised that the text may have been truncated. Yet its comparative brevity is a virtue, for the concentrated intensity contributes to what may be Shakespeare's most horrific work. Other plays are as gory or involve even more murders, but no play is so focused on the act of murder itself, the specific planning and aftermath.

The opening scene establishes the pervasive atmosphere, as the Weird Sisters agree to meet again: "When the hurly-burly's done, / When the battle's lost and won" (1, 1, 3–4). To which battle are they referring? Possibly the immediate conflict in front of them; possibly the battle for the Scottish throne; or, most likely, the battle for Macbeth's soul. The phrase *lost and won* suggests their detachment, while *the set of sun* (1, 1, 5) hints at not only literal darkness but also the death of Duncan, for the sun was traditionally the symbol of the kingship.

When the witches depart, they do so with a threat: "Fair is foul, and foul is fair; / Hover through the fog and filthy air" (1, 1, 12–13). They hereby establish an environment of moral ambiguity and other confusion that envelops not only Macbeth and his wife but also all of Scotland. Trust turns into suspicion, and the country descends into violence and uncertainty, all because of one individual's irresistible urge toward violence.

We hear about this person in the next scene at Duncan's invitation: "What bloody man is that?" (1, 2, 1), and *bloody* sets the tone. The sergeant then reports on the military exploits of "brave Macbeth" (1, 2, 18), who, "Like Valor's minion, carved out his passage / Till he faced the slave" (1, 2, 21–22). The passage emphasizes Macbeth's brutality; he is a killer at heart, despite Duncan's praise: "O valiant cousin, worthy gentleman!" (1, 2, 26). These lines will resound ironically.

The key phrase from the same speech, however, is *Disdaining Fortune* (1, 2, 19). The presence of the witches may suggest that they determine the outcome, but this insertion reminds us that like all Shakespearean figures,

Macbeth is a free agent. Later he tries to explain himself as someone in the grip of fate, but here we are told that he controls his own destiny and is responsible for what happens to him and to others.

How, then, are we to regard the witches? Shakespeare's contemporaries generally believed that witches were in league with the devil and could fly, summon storms, and inflict disease. Perhaps, therefore, these figures should be viewed as invidious meddlers. The outcome matters little to them. They only toy with human vulnerabilities, and as a subject they have chosen Macbeth, whose frailties are exploitable.

In this scene we learn that Macbeth's bravery has earned him the title of Thane of Cawdor because the previous holder of that honor proved a traitor. Duncan gives the order:

> No more that Thane of Cawdor shall deceive
> Our bosom interest. Go, pronounce his present
>   death,
> And with his former title greet Macbeth. (1, 2, 73–76)

As the rhyme of *death* and *Macbeth* rings ominously, Ross replies, "I'll see it done" (1, 2, 77). Subsequently all forms of the word *do* become a motif. Duncan then summarizes the situation: "What he hath lost, noble Macbeth hath won" (1, 2, 78). The line echoes the tone of the witches (1, 1, 3–4), and the sense of instability remains.

When the witches return, so does the word *do*: "I'll do, I'll do, and I'll do" (1, 3, 11). Hearing this line, we realize that doing has three parts: planning, performing, and bearing consequences. Macbeth will be conscious of all three parts but especially the last. The first witch then delineates the punishments she inflicted on a sailor who offended her:

> I'll drain him dry as hay.
> Sleep shall neither night nor day
> Hang upon his penthouse lid.
> He shall live a man forbid. (1, 3, 19–22)

In retrospect, we shall see how all these torments are borne by Macbeth.

A few lines later, Macbeth enters, a distinctive protagonist among Shakespeare's tragic heroes. At the moment he is not royal nor a man overflowing with passion. His only outstanding feature is his skill on the battlefield. In no other way does he prove remarkable, and thus the battle between his ambition and his conscience is one with which audiences may feel uncomfortably close.

His opening line recalls a familiar pattern: "So foul and fair a day I have not seen" (1, 3, 39). Here again is the paradoxical tone of the witches. Later they promise Macbeth the kingship without explaining the steps that he must follow to obtain it, but their ominous appearance shocks Banquo:

> You should be women,

And yet your beards forbid me to interpret
That you are so. (1, 3, 47–49)

This clash of genders is one aspect of the overall theme of unnaturalness.

The witches then greet Macbeth with three titles: Thane of Glamis (his present position), Thane of Cawdor, and King. Banquo comments that the pronouncements leave his friend "rapt withal" (1, 3, 60) and asks the witches to look into the "seeds of time" (1, 3, 61) to project his own future. *Seeds* and *time* both reflect imagery that develops through the play. The first two predictions are both positive and negative, but the third is that he will be the father of kings (1, 3, 70). Banquo dismisses the episode: "Or have we eaten on the insane root / That takes the reason prisoner?" (1, 3, 87–88), but Macbeth is enthralled: "And Thane of Cawdor too. Went it not so?" (1, 3, 91). Once seized by the witches, he never escapes their grip.

Banquo and Macbeth are then joined by Ross and Angus, who bring Duncan's appreciation of Macbeth's victories and also inform him that he has been named Thane of Cawdor. Macbeth is taken aback: "Why do you dress me / In borrowed robes?" (1, 3, 114–15), and his fragmented speech here (1, 3, 125–31) and in the rest of the scene suggests that he wants to tamp down delight that has overtaken him. Banquo issues a warning about the "instruments of darkness" (1, 3, 136), then steps aside to confer with his friends.

Left alone, Macbeth reveals the dichotomy inside him: "This supernatural soliciting / Cannot be ill, cannot be good" (1, 3, 143–44). Although he shares Banquo's trepidation, the rest of this soliloquy confirms that he cannot resist his impulses: "Present fears / Are less than horrible imaginings" (1, 3, 150–51). He will do almost anything to achieve power but is sufficiently respectful of such power that he dares not risk breaking the natural order that buttresses it. Yet he is driven to break it. Yet he fears breaking it. In sum, he is propelled toward an action that terrifies him.

His conclusion is to hope for the best: "If chance will have me king, why, chance may crown me / Without my stir" (1, 3, 157–59). This concession removes Macbeth from the realm of Machiavels (see chapter 4 on *Othello*), including Iago in *Othello* and Edmund in *King Lear*, characters who revel in their own amorality. Macbeth, however, will allow himself to be led by the strongest attraction: "Come what come may, / Time and the hour runs through the roughest day" (1, 3, 163–64). To clarify the feeling, you might ask your students whether they have ever wanted to do something that they knew was wrong yet could not resist it.

In the next scene, which takes place at court, Duncan's first line has ironic overtones: "Is execution done on Cawdor?" (1, 4, 1). He means the former holder of the title, but we foresee when Duncan himself will be killed. His next comment about Cawdor illustrates the king's combination of decency and naïveté: "He was a gentleman on whom I built / An absolute trust" (1, 4, 15–16). He is soon to believe in another deceitful man, Macbeth, whose treachery will vastly exceed Cawdor's.

When Macbeth enters, his praise of Duncan drips with fraudulence (1, 4, 25–30). Indeed, during the next several scenes, while Macbeth anticipates murder, he talks too much, as if hoping that an easy manner will assure everyone that he does not contemplate any dangerous actions. Here Duncan commends Macbeth: "I have begun to plant thee and will labor / To make thee full of growing" (1, 4, 32–33). He promises only good things, then guarantees the same to Banquo, who responds in kind: "There, if I grow, / The harvest is your own" (1, 4, 36–37), invoking more images of growth, which in turn suggest children, a crucial aspect of Macbeth's motivation.

When Duncan names Malcolm as his heir, Macbeth is taken aback but cannot stop contemplating what he dreads: "Stars, hide your fires; / Let not light see my black and deep desires" (1, 4, 57–58). Earlier, Duncan spoke of how "signs of nobleness, like stars shall shine / On all deservers" (1, 4, 47–48). He thinks of the star as beneficent lights, befitting a man with a clear conscience. Macbeth regards them quite differently.

In the opening lines of scene 5, Lady Macbeth clarifies that although she loves her husband, she cannot rely on him:

> Yet do I fear thy nature;
> It is too full o' th' milk of human kindness
> To catch the nearest way. (1, 5, 16–18)

The next word that stands out is *illness* (1, 5, 20), for Lady Macbeth knows that something malignant must lie within someone who intends to fulfill her ambition. Here is another irony, for when the moment of murder is upon her, she proves less bold than her husband. We also note the repetition of *do* (1, 5, 25), with all its implications.

When the messenger brings news of Duncan's later arrival, her first reaction is outrage: "Thou 'rt mad to say it" (1, 5, 36). She seems almost afraid that the messenger can read her guilty thoughts, but when he leaves, her intentions become more terrifying:

> Come, you spirits
> That tend on mortal thoughts, unsex me here,
> And fill me from the crown to the toe top-full
> Of direst cruelty. Make thick my blood. (1, 5, 47–50)

In these and subsequent lines, she reviles her biological femininity and her limited role as a woman, both as part of "nature's mischief" (1, 5, 57). Here again, gender upset contributes to the theme of unnaturalness.

Moreover, she, too, feels the moral horror of what she contemplates:

> Come, thick night,
> And pall thee in the dunnest smoke of hell,

> That my keen knife see not the wound it makes,
> Nor heaven peep through the blanket of the dark
> To cry "Hold, hold!" (1, 5, 57–61)

Like her husband, she is drawn to murder, but her gender dictates that he must be the vehicle through which she gains power.

That her plans will be difficult to fulfill becomes apparent when Macbeth enters. She greets him enthusiastically, but his tentative answers communicate hesitation. She attempts to rouse his determination: "Look like th' innocent flower, / But be the serpent under 't" (1, 5, 76–78). Yet Macbeth still says little: "We will speak further" (1, 5, 83), and although his wife's last line exudes confidence: "Leave all the rest to me" (1, 5, 86), the words prove ironic, for despite her desire to carry out the murder by herself, she will leave the task to him.

Scene 6 maintains the ironic tone, as Duncan admires Macbeth's home:

> This castle hath a pleasant seat. The air
> Nimbly and sweetly recommends itself
> Unto our gentle senses (1, 6, 1–3)

Banquo comments that a bird "Hath made his pendant bed and procreant cradle" (1, 6, 9–10), one more allusion to offspring that Macbeth and Lady Macbeth do not have. What follows is an exchange of polite talk from Lady Macbeth that demonstrates her capacity to "play false," as she earlier indicated her husband should do (1, 5, 22). Meanwhile, Duncan's tributes to Macbeth (1, 6, 25–31) increase the sense of foreboding.

Macbeth's next soliloquy encapsulates his dilemma: "If it were done when 'tis done, then 'twere well / It were done quickly" (1, 7, 1–2). The concept of "doing" as explained here is at the heart of the play. Although Macbeth knows that every act has repercussions, and although he is ruthless enough to plan a murder and callous enough execute it, he is restrained by fear of retribution (1, 7, 7–10). He also emphasizes both Duncan's innocence, as well as Macbeth's own relationship with Duncan: "He's here in double trust" (1, 7, 12). Finally, Macbeth's religious imagery (1, 7, 18–25) confirms that the assassination of the king would be blasphemous, a crime against heaven and the natural order.

All these misgivings, however, cannot withstand the force of Lady Macbeth, who now enters. Before she speaks, Macbeth, as if afraid of her power, stakes out his position: "We will proceed no further in this business" (1, 7, 34). He does not reveal his fears, which she would be unable to answer. Instead he offers a lame excuse (1, 7, 35–38), inviting her to toss it aside, because he wants to be convinced. She does just that.

First she expresses doubt about his love for her, then mocks his manhood:

> Art thou afeard
> To be the same in thine own act and valor

As thou art in desire? (1, 7, 43–45)

Macbeth responds brusquely that he is indeed a man (1, 7, 51–52), but she belittles him further, then in a startling manner dramatizes her own resolve: "I have given suck, and know / How tender 'tis to love the babe that milks me" (1, 7, 62–63). The image that follows of her tearing the baby from her breast suggests terrifying fury.

These lines also raise a familiar question as to the existence of Lady Macbeth's children because none is mentioned elsewhere. Did she have a first husband? We cannot say, but the details may be understood as further evidence of her frustration with womanhood. If her children no longer live, then her greed for worldly power may be interpreted as compensation for failure to carry out what in Shakespeare's time would have been her essential role as a woman. Similarly, Macbeth apparently has no children. Is his hyper-violence on the battlefield an attempt to fill that void?

In any case, as she details her strategy (1, 7, 70–82), her energy convinces him, and he offers what he considers the highest compliment: "Bring forth men-children only" (1, 7, 83), then leaves her with "Away, and mock the time with fairest show. / False face must hide what the false heart doth know" (1, 7, 94–96). *Time* traditionally stands for social stability, and here Macbeth shows his willingness to submit his nation to chaos. His last line, an echo of Lady Macbeth's earlier prediction (1, 5, 20–23), brings out the theme of reality versus appearance.

We next meet Banquo, walking with his son Fleance. Banquo's reflections (2, 1, 7–11) suggest that he, too, is tempted by the witches but unlike Macbeth restrains his desires. When Macbeth appears, Banquo also mentions the Weird Sisters, but Macbeth pretends his mind is elsewhere: "I think not of them" (2, 1, 27–28). We feel him struggling to remain casual, as he does by suggesting that he and Banquo confer later. Perhaps Macbeth still resents the prediction about Banquo's fathering kings.

Left alone, Macbeth muses again about the decision he must make and to which an imaginary knife lures him: "Thou marshal'st me the way I was going, / And such an instrument I was to use" (2, 1, 54–55). He knows that what he plans is wrong, and although his intellect is split, he is willing to follow its dominant instincts: violence and ambition. Meanwhile, his mind runs amok with images of murder (2, 1, 63–74).

Macbeth even makes sound effects work in his favor. Sometimes people trapped in a dilemma allow an arbitrary event to determine the outcome, to stand for a form of destiny. Here Macbeth lets the bell guide him: "Hear it not, Duncan, for it is a knell / That summons thee to heaven or to hell" (2, 1, 76–77). We, however, view the bell as tolling for Macbeth, who will soon descend into his own hell.

The murder itself is carried out with great economy. Having drugged the king's grooms, Lady Macbeth waits anxiously, for she regrets her inability to perform: "Had he not resembled / My father as he slept, I had done 't" (2, 2, 16–17). Possibly he did resemble her father, but she might also have seen him as the father of her nation. Far more likely, however, is that she lacked the courage to kill. She humiliated Macbeth into murder, but gradually she collapses under the knowledge of that act, while Macbeth allows punishment to accumulate. She thus becomes pathetic, while Macbeth accepts the ruin of his life and under that burden becomes tragic.

The differences between them are apparent in the next few lines, delivered breathlessly to reflect the tension of the moment. Macbeth is already haunted by his deed: "I had most need of blessing, and 'Amen' / Stuck in my throat" (2, 2, 43–44). He imagines that he heard "Macbeth shall sleep no more" (2, 2, 57), as if interruption of his own natural order will reflect a greater disruption in nature. In his haste, he even retrieved the daggers that he used to kill, so Lady Macbeth must return them.

Meanwhile, her husband trembles in fear: "Will all great Neptune's ocean wash this blood / Clean from my hand?" (2, 2, 78–79). Lady Macbeth returns to reassure him: "A little water clears us of this deed" (2, 2, 86), a boast that proves breathtakingly ironic. When Macbeth hears the knocking at the door, he immediately regrets his action: "Wake Duncan with thy knocking. I would thou couldst" (2, 2, 94–95). The details of this scene are just one example of why performing this play is so difficult, for the level of hysteria must provoke audience terror but not be so extreme as to incite laughter.

That comes with the presence of the Porter, who follows one dramatic tradition by providing comic relief in the midst of grim circumstances. The Porter identifies himself as guarding "hell gate" (2, 3, 2), then catalogues those who could not gain entrance. All their circumstances apply to Macbeth, but one is particularly close:

> Faith, here's an equivocator
> that could swear in both the scales against either
> scale, who committed treason enough for God's
> sake yet could not equivocate to heaven. (2, 3, 8–11)

The criminals that the Porter describes have allowed ambition to control them, and all end up in despair.

To Macduff and Lennox, the Porter rambles about the similarities between lechery and drink, and as he establishes the addictive powers of both, they may be likened to the role of ambition for Macbeth. It inspired him to action but left him in perpetual hell, as is apparent in Macbeth's next entrance. Macduff greets him, but Macbeth responds in brief, toneless lines, concluding, "'Twas a rough night" (2, 3, 70). He is numb with guilt.

When Macduff returns, his words reveal the magnitude of Macbeth's crime: "Most sacrilegious murder hath broke ope / The Lord's anointed temple" (2, 3, 77–78). The implications of regicide are apparent, and as word spreads, Lady Macbeth and Macbeth reveal their condition. When she is told of the murder, Lady Macbeth responds oddly: "What, in our house?" (2, 3, 103). Even as she tries to evince compassion, she cannot hide her preoccupation with herself.

Banquo corrects her: "Too cruel anywhere" (2, 3, 104). Does he sense something suspicious in her attitude? He seems like a detective observing potential suspects.

Macbeth, meanwhile, broods: "There's nothing serious in mortality / All is but toys. Renown and grace is dead" (2, 3, 109–10). He is gloomy but not because of Duncan; rather, he mourns his own position. Here he pretends to show misery, but by the end of the play he speaks with true bitterness over the meaninglessness of the human condition. Yet even now he does not hide his aspiration. When Donalbain, Duncan's son, rushes in and exclaims: "What is amiss?" (2, 3, 113), Macbeth unleashes cruel wit: "You are, and do not know 't" (2, 3, 114). His delight at drawing closer to the crown cannot be restrained.

When word comes that two grooms were killed as well, Macbeth confesses that in uncontrollable anger he murdered them. Macduff, perhaps already suspecting the truth, asks why, and Macbeth's explanation is excessively passionate: "Here lay Duncan, / His silver skin laced with his golden blood" (2, 3, 130–31). By the time he is finished overstating his case, Lady Macbeth faints. Is she truly overcome? Or does she recognize that her husband is exaggerating his part and acts to draw attention from him?

Banquo urges all to stand together, and Macbeth adds his support: "Let's briefly put on manly readiness / And meet i' th' hall together" (2, 3, 157–58). How ironic that after all of Lady Macbeth's insults about his manhood, Macbeth speaks in such terms. Donalbain, meanwhile, suggests to Malcolm that they separate: "There's daggers in men's smiles. The near in blood, / The nearer bloody" (2, 3, 165–66). He knows that those who have killed once will likely kill again.

Scene 4 dramatizes the political and social ramifications of the assassination. As the murder of the king reverberates throughout Scotland, Ross and the old man describe a series of unnatural phenomena that have occurred (2, 4, 1–24). Macduff enters and remarks that the dead guards may be guilty but refers to them as "Those that Macbeth hath slain" (2, 4, 32), implying that Macbeth was involved.

Macduff also reveals that because Duncan's sons have fled, Macbeth has been named king, but Macduff will not attend the investiture. The old man's warning encapsulates the condition of the country at large: "God's benison go with you and with those / That would make good of bad and friends of foes" (2, 4, 55–56). He offers generosity as well as warning, an appropriate mixture in this volatile environment.

Macduff is not the only one with suspicions, as Banquo clarifies:

> Thou hast it now—king, Cawdor, Glamis, all
> As the Weird Sisters promised, and I fear
> Thou played'st most foully for 't. (3, 1, 1–3)

The rest of the speech shows that Banquo, too, is ambitious but noble enough to resist illegal action. When Macbeth enters and invites him to the installation banquet that night, interspersed into the polite conversation are pointed questions: "Ride you this afternoon?" (3, 1, 21); "Is 't far you ride?" (3, 1, 26); and "Goes Fleance with you?" (3, 1, 39).

The reason for Macbeth's inquiries becomes clear in his next soliloquy:

> To be thus is nothing,
> But to be safely thus. Our fears in Banquo
> Stick deep, and in his royalty of nature
> Reigns that which would be feared. (3, 1, 52–55)

Here Macbeth exceeds the bounds of rationality. The witches foretold that Banquo would sire kings, but now Macbeth, who until this moment has believed their predictions, convinces himself that he can contradict them and thereby possess eternity: "Upon my head they placed a fruitless crown / And put a barren scepter in my grip" (3, 1, 66–67).

Earlier we speculated that Macbeth's failure to procreate intensified his need to prove his manhood in war and by murdering for the throne. Here he confirms that impression: "To make them kings, the seed of Banquo kings" (3, 1, 75). Yet he also shows that he has lost the capacity to distinguish between forecast and inevitability. Killing Banquo's son cannot save the throne for Macbeth's nonexistent children, but the spirit of murder is so imbued in him that he cannot withstand it.

The depths to which Macbeth has fallen are apparent when the two Murderers arrive. They are, we gather, common hoodlums, but now they are Macbeth's kindred spirits and need little convincing to follows his instructions. The second Murderer describes himself:

> I am one, my liege,
> Whom the vile blows and buffets of the world
> Hath so incensed that I am reckless what
> I do to spite the world. (3, 1, 121–24)

Such is an apt description of Macbeth at this moment. Then the other speaks:

> And I another
> So weary with disasters, tugged with fortune,
> That I would set my life on any chance,
> To mend it or be rid on 't. (3, 1, 125–28)

Such will be Macbeth's feelings by the end of the play.

Macbeth tries to soften his directive by explaining his hatred for Banquo, a mutual enemy (3, 1, 132–42), but the terse replies from these two men indicate that they need no persuasion. They kill for money, and this job is simply one more. Macbeth adds one more instruction: "I will advise you where to plant yourselves, / Acquaint you with the perfect spy o' th' time" (3, 1, 148–49). We have no idea who this person is, but we do note that Macbeth reminds his charges to kill Fleance as well, a strange point to leave until the end because Banquo's offspring are the real threat.

By the next scene, Lady Macbeth's conscience has taken hold of her: "'Tis safer to be that which we destroy / Than by destruction dwell in doubtful joy" (3, 2, 8–9). When her husband enters, however, she puts up a courageous front, using familiar words: "What's done is done" (3, 2, 14). Macbeth, though, is inconsolable: "Better be with the dead / Whom we, to gain our peace, have sent to peace" (3, 2, 22–23). And when he reminds her about Banquo and Fleance, she asks another ironic question: "What's to be done?" (3, 2, 50). We feel the world closing in on them.

Macbeth nonetheless feigns bravado and tries to protect her from the worst: "Be innocent of the knowledge, dearest chuck" (3, 2, 51). He then attempts to bolster his own spirits: "Things bad begun make strong themselves by ill / So prithee go with me" (3, 2, 62–63). He has managed to twist his thoughts so badly that the only escape from the burden of evil is to commit further evil.

The next scene is brief but puzzling, as Macbeth's two Murderers are joined by a third. Is this man Macbeth's "perfect spy o' th' time"? To the question of who sent him, he replies, "Macbeth" (3, 3, 2). He also holds the answers to all the questions the others pose. He hears the horses (3, 3, 11), knows Banquo's familiar routes (3, 2, 17–19), recognizes Banquo (3, 2, 21), and realizes that Fleance has escaped (3, 2, 29–30).

Could this man be Macbeth himself? Not likely because Macbeth, as we soon understand, is at the banquet. But can we doubt that this intruder is some aspect of Macbeth? Spiritually he is with his henchmen. He may not commit the killing, but he is the author of the crime and provides all the directives. Therefore his guilt is equal to that of the actual executioners.

At the banquet, Macbeth plays polite host: "You know your own degrees" (3, 4, 1). But his demeanor weakens when the Murderers arrive and quietly boast about Banquo that "My lord, his throat is cut" (3, 4, 18). Macbeth cannot restrain his giddiness: "Thou are the best o' th' cutthroats" (3, 4, 19), but when the men admit that Fleance escaped, Macbeth's satisfaction is diluted: "The worm that's fled / Hath nature that in time will venom breed" (3, 4, 32–33). His manner, though, disintegrates when the Ghost of Banquo enters. Because no one else sees this figure, we may assume that it is subjective, a manifestation of Macbeth's conscience.

In desperation, he confronts it: "Thou canst not say I did it. Never shake / Thy gory locks at me" (3, 4, 61–62). Lady Macbeth tries to bully him: "Are you a man?" (3, 4, 70). When that tactic fails, she seeks to soothe him: "This is the very painting of your fear" (3, 4, 74). The Ghost's constant movement leaves Macbeth terrorized, and he resorts to his most outlandish claim: "What man dare, I dare" (3, 4, 121). Finally, Lady Macbeth dismisses the party with the excuse that the king suffers from some illness.

Left alone with his wife, Macbeth unleashes his panic: "It will have blood, they say; blood will have blood" (3, 4, 151). Yet he maintains sufficient courage to meet the witches and learn more:

> I am in blood
> Stepped in so far that, should I wade no more,
> Returning were as tedious as go o'er. (3, 4, 168–70)

Lady Macbeth offers one solution: "You lack the season of all natures, sleep" (3, 4, 173), but Macbeth refuses to take false comfort: "We are yet but young in deed" (3, 4, 176). He knows that further horrors await.

Scene 5 is regarded by most commentators as an interpolation by another playwright, intended to enhance the atmosphere of dread surrounding Macbeth. It is supplemented by a conversation between Lenox and a nameless lord, both of whom are suspicious of Macbeth's behavior and explanations. When their attention turns to the gathering forces of Macduff, phrases like *most pious Edward* (3, 6, 31) and *the holy king* (3, 6, 34) confirm the divine nature of the kingship. So do the final lines of the scene (3, 6, 51–56), which also clarify the country's pain under Macbeth's rule.

In act 4, Macbeth bursts in on the witches, who are gathered about their cauldron, muttering incantations: "By the pricking of my thumbs, / Something wicked this way comes" (4, 1, 44–45). If the class can handle a momentary diversion, you might ask how many students recognize these lines as book titles. The first is by Agatha Christie, the second by Ray Bradbury. The discussion can then resume with Macbeth's demand for information about the future. No longer does he merely request.

The witches respond by showing him three images. The first is an armed head, which tells him to "Beware Macduff!" (4, 1, 81). The second is a bloody child, who pronounces this threat: "for none of woman born / Shall harm Macbeth" (4, 1, 91–92). Macbeth assumes that now he has no reason to fear Macduff yet still resolves to kill him (4, 1, 93–97). Macbeth is so accustomed to murder that he will kill for the sake of convenience. The child may also represent the children of Macduff who will be slaughtered, as well as all the children who will die in the subsequent war.

The third apparition is the child crowned, who warns that Macbeth is safe "until Great Birnam Wood to high Dunsinane Hill / Shall come against him" (4, 1, 105–7). When the witches' display of eight kings reaffirms that Banquo's children will rule, Macbeth loses control: "Filthy hags, / Why do you show me this?" (4, 1, 130–31). He ignores that he ordered the truth to be revealed, while news that Macduff has fled to England only spurs Macbeth to faster action (4, 1, 166–70). He is so afraid of his conscience that he acts by instinct, not rationality, and the murder of Macduff's family is the first killing for its own sake.

This slaughter is the inevitable outcome of Macbeth's choices. First he murdered in accordance with what he believed the witches had instructed. That act was heinous but with a recognizable goal. Next he worked to subvert the witches by murdering Banquo and attempting to murder Fleance. This last plan, however, is distinct from anything the witches have ordained and, unlike his first two killings, ordered with no moral compunction.

The next scene is the most unbearable in the play because it is the most pointless. Lady Macduff complains that her husband has left her and her children defenseless (4, 2, 8–16), but Ross tries to justify the action: "But cruel are the times when we are traitors / And do not know ourselves" (4, 2, 22). The energy of Macduff's sons is a counterpoint to the crisis that Macbeth has created:

> Then the liars and swearers are fools, for there
> are liars and swearers enough to beat the honest
> men and hang up them. (4, 2, 62–64)

Such is the condition of the world until Macbeth is overthrown.

When the messenger warns her to escape, Lady Macduff's penultimate speech dramatizes the horrors that Macbeth has unleashed:

> I have done no harm. But I remember now
> I am in this earthly world, where to do harm
> Is often laudable, to do good sometime
> Accounted dangerous folly. (4, 2, 82–85)

The subsequent butchery clarifies the nature of Macbeth's rule. This point is the lowest in the play, and whatever sympathy we may have marshalled for Macbeth almost certainly dissolves.

From here, the play turns slowly upward, as Malcolm and Macduff meet. After the previous scene, the latter's comments about the pain his country suffers are tragically ironic: "Each new morn / New widows howl, new orphans cry" (4, 3, 5–6). In the atmosphere of suspicion that grips the country, however, Malcolm is uncertain whether he can trust Macduff and begins to test him by criticizing Macbeth: "You have loved him well. / He hath not touched you yet" (4, 3, 15–16). Neither knows, of course, that Macduff's family has been slaughtered.

After Macduff insists he is loyal, Malcolm apologizes: "Though all things foul would wear the brows of grace, / Yet grace must still look so" (4, 3, 28–30). Here is another example of the contrast between *foul* and *fair*, as well as deceptive appearance. Macduff still mourns the state of his country (4, 3, 39–42) and starts to leave, but Malcolm draws him back with a list of the sins that he will inflict on Scotland: "black Macbeth / Will seem as pure as snow" (4, 3, 63–64).

He details his "voluptuousness" (4, 3, 74) and "avarice" (4, 3, 93–100), then delineates a catalogue of "king-becoming graces" (4, 3, 107) that he disparages but that we should understand as a tribute to King James. Finally, Malcolm promises to reduce Scotland to rubble:

> Nay, had I power, I should
> Pour the sweet milk of concord into hell,
> Uproar the universal peace, confound
> All unity on earth. (4, 3, 113–16)

The image of milk recalls Lady Macbeth's comment that her husband was "too full o' th' milk of human kindness" (1, 5, 17) to murder.

At this boast, Macduff accuses Malcolm of undermining the country that Duncan ruled as a "most sainted king" (4, 3, 127). Only now does Malcolm accept Macduff's fidelity to Scotland, then explains that Malcolm's own innocence was the cause of the deceptions just played (4, 3, 133–56). Macduff's response reflects bewilderment: "Such welcome and unwelcome things at once / 'Tis hard to reconcile" (4, 3, 157–58). Here is one more example of moral disarray.

After the Doctor arrives to learn from Malcolm that Edward, king of England, has furnished ten thousand troops to oppose Macbeth, the Doctor pays tribute to that king, and the pervasive religious imagery (4, 3, 168–81) confirms that all these characters value the alliance between the throne and divine authority. Ross then arrives but resists reporting that Macduff's family has been killed. Under persistent questioning Ross confesses the truth, but Macduff needs time to absorb such horror (4, 3, 240–58).

Malcolm's exhortation that Macduff should "Dispute it like a man" (4, 3, 259) leads to Macduff's statement that he bears responsibility: "Naught that I am, / Not for their own demerits, but for mine" (4, 3, 265–66), and Malcolm's sadness turns into resolution that he must take action:

> Macbeth
> Is ripe for shaking, and the powers above
> Put on their instruments. Receive what cheer you
>   may.
> The night is long that never finds the day. (4, 3, 278–82)

Ripe suggests the reestablishment of the natural order, as does *day* following *night*. After the darkness of Macbeth's reign, light will shine.

In act 5, we see the depths to which Lady Macbeth has sunk. In the Doctor's words:

> A great perturbation in nature, to receive at

once the benefit of sleep and do the effects of
watching. (5, 1, 10–12).

In 2, 2, Macbeth feared he would "sleep no more" (2, 2, 57). Now a similar fate has befallen his wife, as she sleepwalks, reliving the murder in her tormented conscience: "Out, damned spot, out, I say!" (5, 1, 37). And seconds later: "Yet who would have thought the old man to have had so much blood in him?" (5, 1, 41–42), while her language is reduced to childish rhymes: "The Thane of Fife had a wife" (5, 1, 44). Immediately after the murder, she said to Macbeth, "A little water clears us of this deed" (2, 2, 86). Now she mutters, "All the perfumes of Arabia will not sweeten this little / hand" (5, 1, 53–55).

Perhaps most telling, she earlier confidently uttered, "What's done is done" (3, 2, 14). Now her version of that sentiment changes: "What's done cannot be undone" (5, 1, 71). The Doctor summarizes her individual plight that reflects universal disorder: "Foul whisp'rings are abroad. Unnatural deeds / Do breed unnatural troubles" (5, 1, 75–76). Lady Macbeth has retreated into her private hell, and her offstage death will be the literal manifestation of what has occurred figuratively here.

The remainder of the play is structured in several short scenes that reflect the madness of the war. Angus's mention of Birnam Wood recalls the witches' prediction (4, 1, 106), while Lennox speaks of "many unrough youths that even now / Protest their first of manhood" (5, 2, 11–12). Earlier Macbeth tried to assert his manhood by killing Duncan. Now other men are asserting theirs by striving to kill Macbeth. Angus also recalls the imagery of clothing:

> Now does he feel his title
> Hang loose about him, like a giant's robe
> Upon a dwarfish thief (5, 2, 23–25)

Caithness then speaks of purging the state of illness (5, 2, 30–34), and again the sickness of the state reflects Macbeth's condition. Throughout these final scenes, recurrent and familiar imagery intensifies the pressure building around him.

By scene 3, Macbeth borders on incoherence. Recalling spells that have been cast against him (5, 3, 1–11), he dismisses a soldier who brings bad news (5, 3, 17–20). Only in private does Macbeth reveal his emptiness: "My way of life / Is fall'n into the sere, the yellow leaf" (5, 3, 26–27). He understands that he has cut himself from humanity, and such recognition helps give him tragic stature, as does his courage while he dons armor: "I'll fight till from my bones my flesh be hacked" (5, 3, 38). While he urges the Doctor to cure Lady Macbeth, Macbeth's own dialogue grows even more fragmented.

In scene 4, opposing forces unite against him, as Malcolm, now at Birnam Wood, instructs each of his soldiers to "hew him down a bough / And bear 't before him" (5, 4, 6–7). He then assures Siward that of the men who stand with Macbeth, "none serve with him but constrainèd things / Whose hearts are absent too" (5, 4, 17–18). Gradually the stability of the kingdom is being restored.

Macbeth's boldness is briefly evident: "Our castle's strength / Will laugh a siege to scorn" (5, 5, 2–3). Then, however, he hears the wails of women, and these become for him the cries of all mothers who mourn children who have died in the war Macbeth has unleashed: "I have supped full with horrors" (5, 5, 15). He confesses himself emotionally deadened, an admission that prepares him for the announcement by Seyton: "The Queen, my lord, is dead" (5, 5, 19). All Macbeth can say is "She should have died hereafter" (5, 5, 20). *Should* here means "would certainly."

What follows is perhaps the most eloquent expression of hopelessness in literature: "Tomorrow and tomorrow and tomorrow / Creeps in this petty pace from day to day" (5, 5, 22–23). We note the dirgelike rhythm and the simplicity of the language. Once Macbeth sought to possess time; now it rolls by pointlessly, as days blend one into another. The reference to the candle (5, 5, 26) recalls the pervasive imagery of light and dark, and the suggestion of humanity as a player on the stage (5, 5, 27–28) intimates the transitory nature of existence. And as you consider the final line of the speech, you might mention Faulkner's novel *The Sound and the Fury*, narrated in part by the mentally challenged Benjy Compson.

Macbeth is brought back to awareness when a messenger reports:

> As I did stand my watch upon the hill,
> I looked toward Birnam, and anon methought
> The Wood began to move. (5, 5, 37–39)

The apparent fulfillment of the witches' prophesy unnerves him: "To doubt th' equivocation of the fiend / That lies like truth" (5, 5, 49–50). *Equivocation* recalls the words of the drunken Porter (2, 3), but in desperation Macbeth resorts to the attribute that has always been his strongest: courage in battle. Thus as he prepares to die fighting, he orders his troops to rally.

His swagger reasserts itself in the fight with young Siward, but the appearance of Macduff, who swears vengeance for the murders of his wife and child, confirms that Macbeth has not long to live. When they meet, Macbeth boasts: "I bear a charmèd life, which must not yield / To one of woman born" (5, 8, 15–16). But Macduff contradicts him: "Macduff was from his mother's womb / Untimely ripped" (5, 8, 19–20), or by cesarean section. Although Macbeth initially refuses to fight (5, 8, 26), the humiliation of being called "coward" (5, 8, 27) pulls him back:

> Yet I will try the last. Before my body

> I throw my warlike shield. Lay on, Macduff,
> And damned be him that first cries, "Hold! Enough!" (5, 8, 37–39)

He knows that whatever he tries, he is damned, but he leaves with a traditional shout of derision.

The final scene restores stability to the Scottish throne. Macduff enters with Macbeth's head, recalling the three heads that appeared with the witches, then announces that "The time is free" (5, 8, 66). He invokes images of growth: "which would be planted newly with the time" (5, 8, 78), and promises that: "We will perform, in measure, time, and place" (5, 8, 86).

How to sum up this most unlikely of tragic heroes? Virtually every decision he makes, every action he performs, ends up badly. Despite his devotion to his wife, his lack of feeling is appalling. Yet something about him touches us. Perhaps we sense that from the start he is lost: condemned to muddle amid vague promises, the taunts of his wife, his capacity for violence, and his own ambition, all wrapped in a net of uncertainty from which he never escapes.

Afterword

I hope the material here has been useful. As I indicated earlier, I have only introduced our subject, but again, my intended audience is instructors who work with beginners, and experience has taught me that the approaches I've advocated do succeed.

Decades ago, when I was teaching at prep school, I announced to a tenth-grade class that the next book on our reading list was Shakespeare's *Julius Caesar*. Groans filled the room, amid pleas to the effect that couldn't we read something else, *anything* else? A few weeks later, after we finished the play, the same class pleaded to read something else, *anything* else by Shakespeare, and soon we agreed that *Romeo and Juliet* would be ideal. I can't remember a more satisfying moment in my career.

Oh yes. *Romeo and Juliet* was a hit, too.

To conclude, I shall immodestly suggest a few other books of mine that may prove of interest. One is the companion to this volume, *Introducing Shakespeare's Comedies, Histories, and Romances: A Guide for Teachers*. Those interested in the rest of Shakespeare's oeuvre might try *Shakespeare the Playwright: A Companion to the Complete Tragedies, Histories, Comedies, and Romances* (1991). Those who seek commentary about specific themes should look at *The Plays of Shakespeare: A Thematic Guide* (2000), while those interested in the history plays (specifically the Henriad) should read *Political Animal: An Essay on the Character of Shakespeare's Henry V* (2014). Finally, for those who enjoy puzzles and other diversions, I recommend *Bardgames: The Shakespeare Quiz Book* (2011).

Good luck.

About the Author

Victor L. Cahn is professor emeritus of English at Skidmore College, where he taught courses in Shakespeare, modern drama, the history of drama, and expository writing. He also taught at Mercersburg Academy, Pomfret School, Phillips Exeter Academy, and Bowdoin College. He was recently profiled in *300 Best Professors*.

In addition to seven books on Shakespeare, he has written *Beyond Absurdity: The Plays of Tom Stoppard*; *Gender and Power in the Plays of Harold Pinter*; *Conquering College: A Guide for Undergraduates* and the memoir *Classroom Virtuoso* (both published by Rowman & Littlefield); *Polishing Your Prose* (with Steven M. Cahn); and *Walking Distance: Remembering Classic Episodes from Classic Television*. His articles and reviews have appeared in such varied publications as *Modern Drama*, *Literary Review*, *Chronicle of Higher Education*, *New York Times*, and *Variety*.

Dr. Cahn is the author of numerous plays produced Off-Broadway and regionally: *Roses in December*, *Embraceable Me*, *Fit to Kill*, *Dally with the Devil*, *A Dish for the Gods*, *Sheepskin*, *Romantic Trapezoid*, *Villainous Company*, *Getting the Business*, *Bottom of the Ninth*, and *Sherlock Solo*, a one-man show that he performed. Other scripts of his have been presented throughout the Capital Region of New York, where he has taken leading roles in works by Shakespeare, Shaw, Coward, Pinter, Ayckbourn, Simon, Gurney, and Knott.

www.ingramcontent.com/pod-product-compliance
Lightning Source LLC
Chambersburg PA
CBHW020750230426
43665CB00009B/565